Debauchery in the Midwest

Debauchery in the Midwest

Davian

Cover art created by artist John Soukup (kettleart.deviantart.com)

Rev. date: 01/27/2014

To order additional copies of this book, contact:
Xlibris LLC
1-888-795-4274
www.Xlibris.com
Orders@Xlibris.com
540294

TABLE OF CONTENTS

Thank you to my friend that saw my potential and encouraged me to continue writing. He's been there to remind me to keep moving forward even when I was ready to stop. He always knew how to make me smile and find the spark needed to keep going. He has been a great friend and a true inspiration.

I ALWAYS WONDERED

I sit at home thinking of him and I wonder what his cock actually feels like. Will the skin move slightly as I stroke that shaft from the base to the tip? Will the veins begin to bulge before I even begin to stroke and will they become more pronounced as the stroking becomes firmer and faster?

Then I can't help but wonder if the pre-cum will collect quickly because of the strong desire he has for me? Will his jewels react when I take them into my mouth? Will I be able to make him moan with desire? Will he look down to watch my lips consume him or will he tilt his head back, close his eyes and enjoy the moment?

Does he wonder what I taste like? Does he think about how my body will react to his touch? Does he think about what it will be like to hear me whisper my desires into his ear? Does he really know the deep desires I have and is he waiting to hear me tell him about my desires? Will he want to run his fingers through my hair and change that to pulling my hair as the passion becomes more erotic.

Then it happened, to my surprise he showed up at my door unannounced. I opened the door and as he walked in he took my hand in his and he pulled me closer. He put his other hand behind my head as he pulled my hair slightly so I will look up at him as he lowered his mouth to meet mine. His lips were warm as he kissed me. His tongue parted my lips as we begin to kiss. I returned the kiss with passion.

Our hands immediately began to explore each other's body. As his arms wrapped around my back I could feel the strength in his hands as they pressed against me. I do believe that he has been thinking of this moment as much as I have. We kissed for the longest time, holding each other so tightly as if we were both afraid to let go. His tongue was exploring inside my mouth and then pulling out as he began to seductively kiss my lips. He moved his hands and placed them on each side of my face as he tilted my head back and looked into my eyes as he said: "I've always wondered what it would be like to kiss you like that and I have to say I want to do it again". She smiled and suggested that they move into the living room and sit on the sofa so she could shut the door.

He placed himself on the middle cushion and I sat down close to him on his left side. He let out a bit of a sigh then he reached over and grabbed my leg. He pulled it a little as he asked me to sit on his lap. I moved over and was looking deep into his eyes the entire time as I straddled his lap. He placed his hands on my hips and neither one stopped looking into the others eyes. Once I was comfortable he leaned into me and kissed my sweet lips again while he moved his hands up to surround my breasts. As he cupped my breasts I took a deep breath as it surprised me just a bit but I really liked the way it felt. He pressed my ample breasts together then leaned down and gently kissed each breast. I slowly placed my hands on his head as I kissed him. My chest heaving as my breathing became labored with excitement. He licks lightly between my breasts as he looks up into my eyes and asks if he could please see them.

I nodded consent and reached back to unhook my bra as he ran his hands up and under my shirt to unhook it for me. I had on a short sleeved shirt so I was able to pull one strap off of one arm, then the other strap off the other arm. Then reaching up the front of my shirt I pulled the bra off and tossed it onto the floor by the sofa. A part of me wanted to pull my shirt off but I was not proud of the extra weight on my body so I simply pulled my breasts out over the low cut neck line of the shirt.

As both breasts were exposed for him he let out a loud gasp and moaned his pleasure. He wasted no time as he grabbed my right breast and began to suckle that large nipple as if he was a nursing baby. With his lips pressed tight he pulled slightly and released. His hand moved up and he began to roll my nipple between his fingers, licking my nipple and then massaging again. I could tell that he was enjoying himself by the way he was so intently suckling, pinching, and licking my nipples. He was so very gentle and it did feel amazing. However, I wanted him to know it was ok to get just a little rough. I reached up and grabbed the nipple he wasn't suckling and pulled it up firmly. He pulled back and looked up at me as he smiled. He then began to pull a little firmer, nibble a little harder, and my nipples reacted by becoming firmer for him. The room filled with the sounds of my moans from excitement. My body shook lightly as the orgasm began to build. I knew I was going to cum hard if he kept this up. I placed my hands on his upper arms and I squeezed firmly as the orgasm got closer. My breathing became faster, the moans louder and I announced that I was about to cum. I couldn't hold it back, I had to release it. "Don't stop, please don't stop" I said firmly. My hands squeezing his upper arm, he suckled on my breasts with a quest now. He was going to make me cum, he knew this orgasm belongs to him. He started to flick my nipple with his tongue and then it hit. The orgasm was strong as my body began to shake and the orgasm was released. As the climax ended I pulled his head towards my breasts while tilting it so he was placed comfortably between both breasts with his ear resting on my left breast so he could hear my heart beating. I held him close as the orgasm ended, my breathing returned to normal, and my panties so very damp right now. "Oh, baby, that was amazing." I whispered. "Please let me go between your legs and let you release for me now."

He took my face into his hands and kissed me deeply. He pulled me close and held me tight. He went from his deep kiss to sweet quick lip kisses. He gave me a light tap to indicate that he wanted me to get off of his lap. I stood up in front of him, my nipples still hard. I dropped to my knees in front of him. I reached for the button on his jeans to release them but he got there before I did. He unbuttoned his jeans, lowered the zipper, and he stood up to slide his jeans down to the floor. He was wearing very sexy boxer briefs, I could see that he was very firm and that shaft needed to be released. I reached up to the waist band of his briefs and slowly began to lower them. Kissing him softly as each bit was exposed. I reached down and gently took his very hard shaft into my hand as I pulled his briefs down. I was pleased with what I saw, the veins on his shaft were well defined, the head of his shaft was thick with a ridge perfect to get my lips around. His briefs now on the floor and I pull his shaft up a little so I can get compete access to his beautiful sacks. I lick each one and tenderly suck them into my mouth one at a time until I feel his shaft start to twitch in my hand. I asked him to please sit back down on the sofa, I wanted to take his shaft into my mouth.

He sat down, and I moved in between his legs. Gently grasping his shaft and stroking slowly at first from the base to the tip, squeezing off and on along the way. I gradually increase the speed of the stroke. I rub the velvet tip across my warm lips. Then I open my mouth and wrap my lips around the tip. The ridge so well define my lips just naturally fit around it. My tongue flicks across the tip. My mouth lowers down onto his shaft my hand moves down to cup his testicles. I massage them gently while I inch the velvet tip of his shaft across the roof of my mouth and deep to the back of my throat. My breasts began to swing back and forth against his inner thighs as my mouth rides his shaft. He begins to moan lightly as the tip hits the back of my throat. His hands now gently holding my head and lightly stroking my hair and then his hips start to move up and down.

I feel his testicles begin to firm up. His orgasm is getting closer and he rocks his hips a little faster now. He is ready to release in my mouth. His moans have become much louder as he moans my name. I increase the pressure of my lips against his shaft as I now begin to work harder to suck the juices from his shaft.

He enters my mouth deeper with each stroke into my mouth with my hands now on his hips as I try to keep his trusting from going so deep that I gag. He grabs my head firmly now. He lets out a very loud moan as he moans "Yes, Yes, Yes, baby . . . take my cum, drink it". At that moment his shaft started to pulse as his orgasm is released into my mouth. His sack became firm at the same time. The orgasm was amazing. He filled my mouth and I swallowed every last drop. With my head in his hands, as I swallowed the last of his orgasm, he slid off the sofa and sat on the floor facing me. He pulled my face towards him and kissed me deeply. Holding me tightly as if he never wanted to let me go as he said, "I always wondered what it would be like if we allowed ourselves to love each other and I have to say I do like the way that felt." I looked into his eyes and said, "I always wondered the same thing". I kissed him with passion and then laid my head on his shoulder as I cuddled with him.

For that moment I felt so loved. The kind of love that made me wonder what I had done to deserve such tenderness. I hope we do this again. I hope he chooses to enjoy more time with me in the future.

SURPRISE MEETING

She had gone to the bar for a drink after work. Not dressed to meet anyone, but just casual attire and a smile. She was finishing her drink and about to pay her tab when the bartender handed her another drink and said the gentleman at the end of the bar wanted you to have this. Her smile got brighter as she slowly looked to the end of the bar to raise her glass to say thank you. She was pleased to see a very attractive man sitting there raising his glass in her direction, she tilted her head slightly as a way to invite him to come sit by her. As he walked down the bar towards her, he lightly touched her back as he slid onto the bar stool next to her. "Thank you for accepting the drink", he said in an amazing wonderful deep voice. Now that he was closer she could tell he was much younger. She could also see that he had a beautiful smile and an amazingly muscular body. She was flattered but knew he was out of her league.

She thanked him for the drink and asked him if he came here often. She stops by now and then and doesn't remember seeing him before. He explained that he was new in town and this was his first time here. He went on to say how glad he stopped by because it gave him a chance to meet such a lovely lady. She lowered her head and began to blush. He reached for her face, put two fingers under her chin, raised her head and said; "show me that amazing smile again". She looked into his beautiful brown eyes and said; "Thank you for the kind words. I am glad I decided to stop here tonight so I had a chance to me such a handsome man", she said with a smile.

They began to chat, sharing information as she explained she was recently divorced, he was a single man. They both finished their drink and decided to have one more. She didn't want to go there but she needed to make sure he knew she was sure that she is much older than he is. Her suspicions were correct, there was a 13 year difference. But, for some strange reason, it didn't really seem to matter to either of them. She was taken by his smile and kindness, he admitted that he thought she was younger but wanted to continue the friendship. They exchanged phone numbers as they finished the last drink, they hugged as they left the bar and both went their separate ways.

As she drove home she realized she was still smiling. In that short amount of time he had made an impression on her, she was hoping he would call or text soon. She knew she wouldn't be the one to call first, she would wait to hear from him.

To her surprise, a text from him came through later that night that simply read; 'Sweet dreams. I hope you give me a chance to see you again soon'. She didn't want to seem too eager so she didn't respond right away. But, after about 15 minutes she replied by sending a text that read, 'sweet dreams to you my new handsome friend. I enjoyed meeting you tonight and we should make plans to meet again sometime soon'. She then went to bed, with a smile on her face, excited about the connection that was made tonight.

The next day he sent her another text wishing her a day of smiles. At that point she figured that he knew the age difference, he knew she didn't have a bikini body, so why not take it a step further so she replied with a text and made the first move. She asked him if he would like to go out for supper after work some night this week. She told him she wasn't fond of seafood but he could pick the place. Then she got herself ready for work and started her day.

During his first break at work he replied and suggested they meet tonight at a local steak house at 6:00. She wasn't expecting it to be so soon but why not, she agreed. This gave her enough time to get home and change into appropriate clothing. She accepted his suggestion and was so excited for the rest of the day.

She leaves work right at 5:00 and rushes home. She pulls on a pair of fairly new jeans and a light weight shirt that is sexy but appropriate. Fixes her hair, brushes her teeth and she is ready to go. She can't believe she's going out to dinner with a man so much younger, but is looking at it as you can never have too many friends.

He was already there when she arrived, he had made reservations so they were seated right away. He was quick to compliment her and tell her how beautiful she looked, she thanked him and told him he looked mighty fine himself.

The waiter same over, took their order and then they began to share stories about the day. He told her he was glad she didn't mind the age difference and hoped they could become good friends. She looked at hum and smiled. She was thinking the same thing but hoped they would become more then friends.

They finished their meal and he reached across the table and held her hand. She looked into his eyes and smiled. She was unsure how to react but she knew she wasn't going to pull her hand away. Then he spoke, "would you like to go back to the bar where we met and continue talking for awhile before we call it a night? I want to know more about you if you don't mind".

She gave his hand a light squeeze and told him she would like to do just that so she could find out more about him.

The waiter brought the bill and they both reached for it. He was faster and said, "oh no, this is on me." He paid the bill and as they slid out of the booth he took her hand as they walked out to the parking lot. He walked her to her car, opened the door for her, leaned in and gave her a soft kiss and said he would meet her at the place they met. He waited to make sure her car started and everything was fine before he went to his own car. She couldn't believe he was such a gentleman, she hasn't been treated like this in a long time and she liked the kindness.

Soon after she drove away he called her and told her to go ahead and get a booth for them, he had to make a quick stop and he would be there soon. So she went on in, asked for a booth, and waited. It didn't take him long to get there and to her surprise he was holding a beautiful bouquet of flowers. He walked up to the booth, leaned over to hand them to her and gave her another sweet kiss. She couldn't stop smiling now. To her surprise he sat in the booth right next to her and slid over kind of close. He asked her what she wanted to drink and she said a beer would be fine. He ordered two beers and he turned to look at her as he put his arm around her shoulders. She slid her hand down and placed it on his upper thigh as she looked at him and smiled. "Well, you don't waste any time do you?" she asked. She went on to say; "I like a man that isn't afraid to show his feelings." He reached his hand up towards her face, placed his hand on her cheek, turned her head towards him and kissed her with passion. As the kiss became firmer she found herself applying pressure to his upper thigh with her hand. When the kiss was done they saw that the waiter had brought their beers, they didn't realize anyone came back to the table.

They both took a drink of their beer and in an effort to slow things down a bit she started to make small talk. She asked him where he worked and what his plans were for his future. Turns out he works for a large company and was sent here to head up a new satellite office in the area and he planned to make this small town his home. She was happy to hear he had a good job and that he planned to stay here and wasn't planning to leave in a few months. He went on to tell her he hopes that their friendship will grow.

They kept on talking and they kissed a few more times as they finished their beers. She was tempted to ask him over to her house but they both have to work tomorrow and she thought it was too soon. So, instead she said; "as much as I wish this evening could last much longer we both have to work in the morning so perhaps we should call it a night soon."

He agreed and replied with; "I do hope we will see each other again. I find you to be a very interesting woman. I do want to spend more time with you." So they agreed they would keep in touch and make plans to meet again very soon.

They left the bar and once again he walked her to her car. This time he pulled her close as he kissed her and his hands roamed across her back. Her breathing became heavy, he knew how to kiss. He knew how to make her melt in his arms. She thanked him again for the flowers then she got into her car. As she drove away she knew this relationship was going to be enjoyable for both of them. She also knew she wanted to be with him in a more intimate way.

She put the flowers in a vase as soon as she got home and just looked at them and smiled. He was so taken by this young man, she decided that she was ready to invite him to her place for a dinner. She wasn't the best cook but certainly she could find something to make that they could both enjoy. But, she didn't want to seem too eager so she didn't suggest it too quickly, she was going to wait for him to contact her. It wasn't going to be easy to wait but she was determined. She did, however, send him a text to thank him for a wonderful evening and again for the flowers.

What she didn't know was that he was feeling the same was as he was driving home. As soon as he got the text he pondered on what he should do. He wanted to invite her to his place so they could chat in an area with no interruptions and he also wanted to be able to become more intimate with her. He was afraid he would be moving too fast for her, understanding that she was recently divorced and may not be ready for the way he wanted to treat her. He saw her text and he wasted no time. He took a deep breath and was hoping she wouldn't run because he was moving so fast. He began to text; "I too had a wonderful time and would like to see you again. Would you like to come to my place for dinner? I hope I am not moving too fast but all I can think about it seeing you again." Then he pressed 'send' and hoped it was received well.

When the text appeared on her phone she let out a squeal of joy. She didn't waste any time, she quickly replied with a strong "YES, I would really enjoy spending more time with you and dinner at your place seems like the perfect place."

They exchanged text messages and decided on a date, he gave her directions to his place, and they both had a couple of days to prepare.

Over the next couple of days they exchanged text messages and the desire to become intimate was made clear from both of them.

The day finally arrived and she was so excited. She had picked out the perfect outfit that was casual but yet sexy. She left work a little early just to give her hair a little extra attention and then she was ready to go to his place. With the address programmed into the GPS of her car she headed in his direction. She arrived and he walked out the front door to meet her. As she parked the car he was right there, opening her door and he extended his hand to help her out. As she stood up he pulled her closer, kissed her then gave her a hug as he told her how beautiful she looked. He took her hand and they walked into his place. It was very clean and whatever he was cooking smelled amazing. He handed her a glass of wine and he raised his glass to toast. "Here's to a long lasting friendship" then they gently tapped their glasses and took a drink. Dinner was ready and he pulled a beautiful lasagna with warm bread sticks out of the oven. It was served with some sweet corn he had just cut off the cob and a nice toss salad. They exchanged small talk as they ate, finished their glasses of wine and were starting on their second glass when the meal was done. Instinctively she stood up to gather the dirty dishes and take them to the sink but he was quick to take her hand and tell her he would take care of it later. He took her by the hand to the living room and they sat side by side on the sofa. He put his arm around her, leaned over and kissed her cheek. Her hand resting on his upper thigh.

Then, without warning, he made his move. He took her face in his hands, turned her head towards him, and he kissed her with more passion than she has felt in years. She was melting in his arms, he is an amazing kisser. One of his hands slid down from her face and found its way to her ample breast where he softly caressed her slowly. He was pleased that she did not pull away but instead moved her hand up from his thigh to his bulging crotch.

His kisses moved from her lips, down her neck, and he had pulled her breast from her shirt and he met that firm nipple with his lips. He was pleasantly surprised to find that she had very large suckable nipples. Her head tilted back as she let out some light moans of delight. He had taken over her every thought as he suckled her nipple, she couldn't even concentrate enough to massage that wonderful shaft that was growing in his pants. He pulled his mouth away and looked up at her face and saw the joy. He kissed her again and she put her arms around him and roamed across his back. As they hugged she told him she would like to take his pants off, her intent was to make him moan with pleasure.

Without missing a beat he stood up and held his arms out as he said; "come get it baby, release the monster".

She unbuttoned and unzipped his jeans and slowly slid them down to the floor. She gasped as she saw the bulge in his boxer briefs. She put her fingers inside the waist band and slowly slid them down, pulling them at the front to allow that monster to come out. She had his clothes on the floor and helped him to step out of them. She turned him around, sat him back down on the sofa, and she went to her knees where she took that shaft gently in her hand and raised it to her lips. Her mouth open she licked the tip and around the ridge and began to slowly take him into her mouth. The head was silky smooth, the ridge well defined. She took the tip into her mouth then pulled back up, repeating that a few times. Then she took a little more into her mouth then licked back up to the tip massaging with her lips along the way. He was running his fingers through her hair as she took him in. He let out the sounds of pleasure and encouraged her every move by telling her how wonderful it felt. She felt his veins start to thicken, his shaft becoming even firmer, his balls were firming up in her hand. She knew she could get him to release in her mouth if he would allow her to continue.

He had other plans, he gently pulled her head back and told her he would like to take her clothes off and feel her skin next to his in the bedroom. She wasn't about to say no, at this point her juices were already flowing, her breathing was heavy. She agreed as she kissed the tip before standing up. He stood up at the same time, gently pulled her close and held her in his arms for just a minute. He reached down and unfastened her pants and let them fall to the floor. He was surprised and pleased to find that a woman her age wore sexy thong panties. He pulled her panties down and was even more surprised to see she wasn't shaved but she was front to back smoothly waxed. As he pulled her close for another tender hug his shaft slid smoothly between her legs. He felt the moisture between her legs, she felt his shaft twitch. He took her shirt in his hands and pulled it up slowly then over her head. He kissed her as he reached to the back and released her bra and slid the straps down her arms and let it fall to the floor. She then pulled his shirt up, her hands gliding along the side of his body as then up his arms as she pulled the shirt over his head.

They held each other close feeling their bare skin, that had been concealed buy clothes these three days, touching for the first time as they kissed with passion. Their tongues were exploring as they kissed. Both of them were moaning lightly with pleasure as their hands started to massage across their backs and down their waist. His skin was so smooth, everything felt so amazing. He enjoyed her healthy curves then he took her hand and without saying a word he led her to the bedroom.

He pressed her back against the bed, grabbed her hips and lifted her slightly so she was sitting on the edge of his bed. He put his hands on her shoulders and gently laid her back onto the bed, her legs hanging down over the edge. He put his hands under her legs and pulled them up, pressing her knees towards her breasts and exposing her warm pussy. With precision he pressed the head of his still hard long shaft against her opening. He leaned forward, with his hands massaging her breasts he looked into her eyes and smiled as he asked her if she was ready to be pleased. She nodded and smiled, her hips moved slightly trying to press in him inside her. Then he softly said; "Patience baby, I want this to last for both of us."

He gently pressed his cock into her pleasure box. The tightness surprised him as he forced the head in stopping just as the ridge entered. "you're very tight baby", he said with a devilish smile. He then pushed in further, one inch at a time, watching her reaction as he entered her. Her body arched, her chest expanding with gasps of pleasure. His hands on her hips and then they both felt it, his cock totally inside her with his jewels pressed against her body. Her muscles began to grab onto his shaft providing a massage that was coating him with silky juices. Her hips couldn't be still any longer and she began to rock up and down.

At that point he couldn't hold back, his cock was reacting to the massage her pussy muscles were providing. With his hands on her hips he began to thrust. Long slow thrusts at first but as her screams of pleasure became louder he started to move faster. Pushing in deep with each thrust. Her juices were flowing and with each thrust the juices were splashing against him. He began to moan with each thrust, fucking her with such passion. His thrust speeds up and she screams out her joy. He becomes vocal about his pleasure as his hands grab her hips more firmly. He announces, "oh, baby, I am going to fill you up . . . ooooh, baby!"

Her body tightens and begins to twitch as her orgasm is released. Her inner muscles grabbing hard against his cock as her juices explode. His body tightened as his cock began to pulse and twitch as he filled her with his warm protein filled juices. As the last drop was released he leaned forward, kissed her large nipples, moved up and kissed her neck, then laid his head on her chest.

His exhausted cock began to shrink inside her and slowly began to slip out of her. "Don't go too far baby. I want to suck your cock now so I can taste your juices mixed with mine", she whispered. He smiled as he pushed her totally onto the bed. He crawled up and lay next to her and she rolled over and began to lick his cum covered cock. The juices were sweet and thick as she took his now soft cock into her mouth. Then moving down and licking his sweet covered jewels. When she properly cleaned him up she moved up and lay next to him. Her arm draped over his chest as she cuddled next to him.

"You are an amazing woman"; he breathed. "The way your muscles grabbed onto me was incredible. I do hope we can do this again and often"; he said right before he kissed her.

"You, my friend, are an amazing man. I am sure we will be seeing a lot more of each other in the near future", she said and then she gave him a tender kiss as her hand massaged his chest.

This was even better than she could have hoped for. That night they met in the bar is going to change both of them. They will find happiness in each other arms.

HIDE-N-SEEK

As she arrived at her desk she was surprised to find an envelope with her name on it had been placed on her chair. She knew it was from him because of the cute heart shapes drawn on the envelope. She pulls the envelope to her face and smells his scent and smiles. He is so kind to her, he is a special friend.

She opens the envelope and is unsure of the message that read: "I know you have an appointment over lunch today, please ask the receptionist if she has a message for you." Well, the note was correct; she regularly went to get an allergy shot once a week. Although she never looked forward to this event, today was different. She was looking forward to her next message. She tried to send him an email but he ignored her with a smile, he knew she would love this journey.

Finally, it was time to go to her appointment. She walked a little faster to her car than on any other day. As she checked in for her appointment she asked if they had a message for her. Yes, they did have a message and she was given another envelope. Similar to the one she received earlier, decorated with great pictures. She was curious but waited until after she got her shot and was sitting in the waiting room. She opened it carefully and read another note that simply read, "Today, for your lunch, you will go to the sandwich shop next door and ask for a #4 Special. They will have your favorite sandwich ready along with another note. I do hope you are smiling today; you are so pretty when you smile. Enjoy my friend."

As soon as she was done sitting for the mandatory 15 minutes after the shot she quickly left and headed to her sandwich shop to get the next direction. She pulled up to the drive thru to place her order and after the normal comment from the person on the inside she simply said . . ."I'd like the #4 Special". To her surprise the person responded back calling her by her name. She had a big smile on her face when she drove up to the pick-up window. She had ordered here enough she knew how much money to have ready and she handed it to the guy at the window. He smiled and told her that her lunch had been paid for. She put the money back into her purse as he handed her a sandwich, soda, chips, and another note. Wow, she usually just got a sandwich so this was a bonus. Now, the test, did he know what kind of soda she liked. Ok, the truth is she would like it no matter what it was but yes, he got it right and ordered a diet coke for her.

She pulled past the window so she could open and read the new note that was placed in an envelope with fancy hearts drawn on it. The note reads, "I do hope you are having a great day my friend. I wish I could see the smile on your face as you open each of these notes. I can only hope that these notes are making you smile widely. I want this smile to be with you all day and when I come to your place after work I hope you will great me at the door with a smile. xx".

A single tear fell from her eye as she read the note. She hadn't had a man give her attention like this for a very long time, she was taken aback by his kindness and really didn't know what to expect after work.

She drove back to the office and everyone noticed the smile on her face and several commented on how radiant she looked throughout the day. She even walked with a little extra pep in her step that afternoon.

Then, at 4:00 a co-worker that sits in her area handed her another envelope! She opened the envelope and this note read, "I will bring pizza for supper, be prepared for a fun evening. I will see you shortly after work. Keep smiling!" Her co-worker asked if she was ok and she replied with a smile as she said, "I am more than ok. Someone has helped me find my smile. All of a sudden I feel like the homely girl that just got asked to prom by the star quarterback." Then she asked her co-worker if he said anything when he dropped off this note. She smiled and told her that the envelope was on her chair this morning with a note asking if she could please deliver it at 4:00.

At the end of the day she left on time and went straight home. She quickly got out of her work clothes and put on some comfortable jeans and a zip-up sweatshirt. She was secretly hoping he got pizza that doesn't have onions on it. You know, just in case there might be a kiss she didn't want to have onion breath. She put some plates out for supper and waited patiently.

Finally, the knock on the door, her heart skipped a beat. She quickly opened the door, welcomed him to her home, took the pizza and set it on the table, then took his coat and hung it in the closet. After she shut the closet door and turned around he took her arm, looked into her eyes, and asked if she had a good day. With a playful giggle she acknowledged it was an incredible day and she thanked him for each note. As she was looking into his eyes thanking him for the great day he took his hand, placed it behind her head, and kissed her gently. Then he stepped back and said, "Let's eat before it gets cold, I got your favorite."

She was a bit in shock; they didn't have a relationship so she did not anticipate a kiss. This was a welcome surprise. He sure did get her favorite; he had obviously paid attention to things she had told him. They went to the table and sat across from each other and ate some wonderful pfizza. They each had a single beer with the meal. When they were done, together they stacked the plates in the sink, wrapped up the left overs and put them in the fridge.

He then took her hand and took her to the sofa where he sat down next to her with his arm around her shoulder. She relaxed and her head lay on his shoulder, she tilted her head, looked up at him, and thanked him for the incredible day and the wonderful supper. She told him she didn't know what she had done to deserve his kindness but she was very grateful for each minute. He lowered his head, kissed her forehead and told her that he loves to make her smile. He gave her a bit of a squeeze and held her tight.

She was working hard to contain her desire because she wasn't sure if he wanted more than the friendship they had created. She loved their friendship and sure didn't want to lose it. But for right now, she wanted to kiss him.

He gave her shoulder a squeeze; he really wanted to kiss her but didn't want to risk losing such a great friend. He saw the remote and reached for it and found a music channel. Then the room was filled with soft music. He gave her shoulder a firm hug; he turned towards her, put his other hand on her chin and kissed her. She was surprised by the action, he was so happy she immediately returned the kiss. She reached her arms around him and kissed him with all the passion she had been holding back. They embarrassed this kiss and their tongues danced. She began to moan softly.

Their lips parted, he leaned back slightly and ran his fingers through her hair. He looked into her eyes and said, "Oh, baby, I hope I didn't go too far. Your friendship means the world to me; I hope I didn't just cross the line. I will stop if you are uncomfortable."

Without thinking twice, she turned towards him, she straddled his lap, held his face in her hands and looked into his eyes when she said, "don't stop now baby, this feels too good. Our friendship is strong and I don't want this to stop."

His puts his hands on her shoulder and pulls her back towards him. She leans him and they begin to kiss again. Their passion was intense, they were falling in love.

His hands moved down and slid under her shirt. When his hand touched her skin she gasped lightly. His hands moved to her back and massaged her lightly. He unhooked her bra and then moved his hands towards the front and began to massage her ample breasts. Her breathing became heavy, she didn't want to stop kissing but she couldn't continue. Her head tilted back and she let out a moan. "Oh, baby, you are incredible. You are going to make me cum. My breasts are so sensitive and you know how to touch them. Please let me drop to my knees and allow me to feel your shaft in my mouth."

He gave her breasts a firm squeeze as he nuzzled her neck with kisses. He put his hands on her waist so she wouldn't fall as he stood up. He took her hand and led her to the bedroom. It was obvious this was going to turn into something wonderful.

As they entered the bedroom he unzipped her sweatshirt. Her bra still unhooked from earlier fell off her shoulders. This was the first time he saw her bare breasts and he was taken aback by the beauty of her large nipples. He was quick to grab her right breast and lower his mouth so his lips could wrap around her nipple. Oh my, his warm mouth sucked it in as his tongue flicked her now firm nipple. Her hands holding his head as he suckles her breast. Her head tilted back as she moans out her joy as the way he is making her feel.

She reaches down towards his waist band to remind him of what she asked for. He reluctantly stopped suckling and let her take over. As he leaned back and stretched out his arms to give her full access she looked into his eyes and smiled. She began to unbutton his jeans then unzip them. She gently slid her hand down the front of his pants and felt his shaft, already starting to become firm. Her thumb rubbed across the smooth velvet tip. She began to slide his jeans down and then, with her hands along the waistband of his briefs she stretched them to glide over his now fully engorged penis. As it was released she took a deep breath and moved to her knees. It is beautiful, the ridge is well defined and the veins beginning to become more predominate. Her hand gently grabs his shaft; she opens her mouth and directs the tip to glide across her tongue. She then wraps her lips around his tip and slowly takes it in. Once the ridge is past her lips she begins to glide her tongue across the tip. He looks down and watches as she takes each inch into her mouth. His hands now down and placed gently on her head. As her lips reach the base and the tip hits the back of her throat, she takes a deep breath and begins to ride his shaft. Slowly moving up, massaging his shaft with her lips all the way up. When back at the tip her tongue glides over the top and she takes the length of the shaft into her mouth again. Slowly at first but she starts riding his shaft quickly. She was, at this point, ready to feel his shaft throb for her and fill her mouth with his love. Her hands now on his hips, keeping him steady as she sucked harder and faster. She begins to moan loudly as she starts to feel his shaft tighten up. He was about to cum for her. The room began to smell of sex as her own orgasm hit hard. He joined her in moans of pleasure as his shaft started to throb harder. "I am going to fill your mouth baby; I hope you are ready for this . . . . aaaahhhhhh . . . Oh, baby, you are incredible". She felt his warm cum hit the back of her throat and then, in spurts, filled her mouth with his salty love. She swallowed every bit. When his orgasm was complete she stood up, wrapped her arms around him and pushed him back onto the bed where she wrapped herself around him. Holding him close as their bodies began to relax.

Their friendship became stronger that day. She was looking forward to sharing so much more with him.

REUNITED

When reunited with an old friend she found that his hugs were just as powerful as they were when they were in High School. His kisses still took her breath away with the passion he puts into each one. She knew he still had the power to make her moan with desire.

She invited him in to sit down so they could chat and catch up on what has happened since they saw each other last. They shared stories that made each other laugh and he realized how much he enjoyed her laughter and she enjoyed his laughter too.

He reached out and took her hand in his and he looked deeply into her eyes as he told her how much he has missed her over the years and how happy he was they have reconnected. He went on to express his love of her laughter and how enlightening it is to see her enjoy their time together.

Then, without warning, he leaned over and kissed her lightly. Then he sat back to wait for her reaction. She turned towards him and smiled. Then she stood up, stood right in front of him, then she straddled his lap, took his face in her hands, looked into his eyes. With a smile she said to him; "baby, that isn't how we kissed when we were in High School" and then she opened her mouth slightly as she kissed him as her tongue darted around inside his mouth. His arms wrapped around her waist and he pulled her close. The two were kissing as if they were 17 again.

She could feel that her juices were flowing. Her nipples becoming firm. His shaft was becoming very thick and he wanted to release it from his pants. He pulled back and stopped kissing her to ask her if he could see her sweet tits again. He remembered that she had the firmest nipples he had ever seen and they stuck out so beautifully.

"Oh, baby, you always did like my nipples. I have taken very good care of them" she said as she began to pull her shirt up over her head. She heard his gasp as her shirt was removed. She was wearing a bra that had holes in the front to allow an opening for her nipples. There they were, right in front of is face, just as perky and firm as he remembered them. He didn't even wait for her to remove her bra, he quickly took her left nipple into his mouth pulling it out past the edge of her bra and suckling on it as if he was a nursing baby. He began to moan slightly as he suckled, putting his arms around her and pulling her close. She put her hands on his face and pushed his head back as she leaned the other way. She looked into his eyes as she reached around her back and unhooked her bra so he could have full access to every inch of her ample breasts. She stood up, removed her bra then reached for his hand and pulled him up. She dropped her bra on the floor and pressed her breasts against him as she firmly kissed him. She hugged him tightly and whispered into his ear asking him if he would allow her to remove his jeans. He whispered back a simple response asking if she would like to also remove her pants so their naked bodies could be pressed together.

She took a deep breath and reminded herself that he doesn't have the football player body he had in High School, certainly he will understand that she doesn't have her High School body either. As she began to remove her jeans, she turned her back to him so when she bent over to push her jeans to the floor he would see her firm, but round, ass. She was wearing a pair of orange thong panties and as soon as he saw her bend over he very loudly said; "NICE"!

He had dropped his jeans down to his ankles and when he saw her bent over he quickly stepped out of his jeans and moved towards her before she stood up. He grabbed her hips and pressed his hard, thick, shaft against her ass cheeks. He angled his hips to direct that firm shaft to glide between her legs. He knew he would love to dip into her sweet ass but felt that since they had not talked about that he wouldn't start there. He really did like what he saw, she was just as beautiful as he remembered.

All of a sudden they both felt like two 16 year olds. She let out a playful squeak when he pressed against her and she found herself pushing back against him. With his hands on her hips he held her firm as he pressed against her slowly moving back and forth. He could feel the warmth from between her legs. She could feel the tip of his shaft pressing between her swollen lips.

He reached around her, took her arm in his hand and turned her around. He took her face in his hand, lifted her chin, and kissed her deeply. He wrapped his arms around her so he could embrace her as they kissed. His hand roaming along her back, she was rubbing his back at the same time. He sound of their passionate moans filled the room.

His shaft still very hard and pressed against her abdomen as they kissed. She could feel the silky moisture of his precum forming on the tip. He put his hands on her shoulders and directed her to the hallway and asked her to take him to the bedroom. He made it clear to her that he wanted to make love to her.

She moved quickly to the bedroom, she wanted to feel him deep inside her, she wanted to make love to him also. As soon as they got there she bent over to lick those juices from the tip of his shaft. She pushed him back so he could lay down on the bed. He got himself centered on the bed, she crawled on between his legs. Her hand gently cups his testicles as her tongue circled the silky smooth tip.

He remembered how she used to work her mouth on his shaft back when they were in High School. He reached down and grabbed her head as she wrapped her lips around his tip. He pulled lightly asking her to slide up his body and straddle his shaft. She couldn't help herself, she pushed his hands away as she opened her mouth, and took the entire length of his shaft into her mouth. The tip was hitting the back if her throat. She slid her tongue along the back side as she lifted her head. Then she moved up, straddled his body as he directed his long, thick, shaft into her warm and wet pussy.

With his hands on her waist he lowered her down. They were looking into each others eyes, he saw the way her eyes widened as his shaft pressed into her warm opening. She bit her lower lip as she felt his jewels press against her. She bent over, kissed him, and then started to rock her hips up and down. Her juices were flowing, they could hear the sound of the wetness as he thrust deep into her. Then he suddenly grabbed her hips and held her still. He was about to cum and didn't want this to end so soon. He pushed her over onto her back. Her legs spread wide as he lifted her legs and pressed them up towards her shoulders. Her wet pussy right there for his to see. He teased her just a little by rubbing the tip of his shaft across her firm and swollen clit. She starts to moan with pleasure, he can see that her pussy is pulsing and he pressed his tip into her. Then, with one quick thrust, he started to move in and out. Her hips rocking to meet his.

It didn't take long, his body became stiff, he let out a very loud moan as he filled her with his seed. At the same time her pussy was throbbing as her orgasm hit.

He then laid on top of her, kissing her repeatedly. He rolled off to the side and they held each other. She excused herself, asked him to stay right there. She went to the bathroom and got a warm wash cloth. She returned to lick him clean, followed by using the warm wash cloth. They continued to lay in the bed and chat while enjoying the feeling of their bodies touching.

SHE WAS FEELING ALONE

She had been feeling kind of alone lately. The weather has been a bit chilly and the sky was kind of gray. She was just enjoying a day of relaxation as she sat on the sofa when there was a knock at the door.

She ran her fingers through her hair to make it look somewhat decent before she answered the door. She looked through the peek hole in the door and was so surprised to find her friend standing there. He had a smile on his face as she opened the door.

"It is good to see you my friend. What brings you to my neck of the woods today?" She asked. He took a step forward and walked in, closing the door behind him.

"We'll I'm in this neck of the woods because I wanted to spend some time with you. I do hope you don't mind me just stopping by." He said with a smile. He reached towards her, put his arms around her and gave her a gentle hug.

She took a deep breath, his hug felt incredible; she didn't expect that because he just isn't the hugging type. She looked into his eyes, smiled, and reminded him that he was welcome at her home at any time.

He took her hand and then went to the sofa and sat down. He looked at her and let her know he thought it would be a great day to talk and get to know each other a little better. He also mentioned that perhaps a hug here and there would be appropriate.

She relaxed on the sofa, making herself more comfortable and turning slightly towards him so she was ready to hear all her friend had to say.

He placed his hand on her knee, giving it a gentle squeeze. "We'll, I've been a little worried about you. I know this has been a rough time for you and since I've never been through it myself I probably don't understand what it is like for you. How you are doing and be honest about the good and bad of it all? Talk to me my friend, don't hold anything in"

Wow, she didn't see his coming at all. But she also knew she needed to talk about how she was feeling, the loneliness and she felt that nobody understood. She turned herself so she was facing front and not facing him but he grabbed her knee and asked her to turn back towards him. He reminded her that he wanted to see her eyes as she spoke to him.

She took a deep breath and tried to think of the best place to start, she didn't want to say things that would make her look weak because she really is a strong woman. Then she placed her hand on top of his and started to talk. She told him how she felt that the many months since her husband sent her to be on her own she really missed being touched, hugged, and most of all being kissed. She missed having someone to talk about her day when she came home from work. She was afraid she would never be able to find anyone that would love her and hold her the way she wants to be loved. Her eyes started to fill with tears; she didn't want him to see her like this. She lowered her head and tried to pull it together then he gave her hand a gentle squeeze and said, "it's ok my friend, let it out, share this with me, I am here for you."

She squeezed his hand rather firmly, she was afraid to go on but she took another deep breath, looked up at him and told him how she didn't miss the stress she left behind, she didn't miss the fact that he never made her feel pretty and she hoped that she could heal from how he made her feel she would never be pretty enough. He reached over and grabbed her tissue from the end table. He patted the tears away for her. He could see she was in pain. Not actual physical pain but deep emotional pain. He felt bad he didn't know about this earlier because he does think the world of her and he thinks she is a beautiful woman.

She went on to say how she missed having someone to enjoy a movie with, she would love to have someone playfully slap her ass as she walked by, and she would enjoy having someone to kiss her for no reason—just a kiss out of the blue. She missed being touched, she missed affection.

He took his hand from her knee and put it on the side of her head and pulled himself closer so he could press her head against his chest. He ran his fingers through her hair and apologized for not seeing her pain, he didn't want her to feel alone. He held her close so she knew he cared.

With kindness in his voice he said to her; "My friend, I am here for you. Please don't hold this in any more. Let me help you through this tough time."

Then he took his forefinger and lifted her chin slightly as he slid his hand along the side of her face. His thumb stopping just before her ear as his fingers reached to the back of her head. Then he leaned over slightly and nibbled on her lip and kissed her lightly. They exchanged several soft kisses. His hand left her chin and he embraced her head, entwining his fingers in her hair as he kissed her with passion. He then wrapped his arms around her, kissed her forehead, and held her tightly.

She felt so cared for at that minute. She was so glad he let her unload like that. She never expected him to show her affection and she knew it wasn't from him heart but it was much needed for her to be able to move forward. He helped her in a way that he may never understand. She prays he never feels the pain she has felt. For now, she continues to enjoy his hugs, his kisses, and his attention.

She will survive this time in her life and she will come out of it a stronger and better woman for it.

HER FIRST TIME

He talked about his desire to share this experience with her. But she didn't want to admit that she had never done it. It isn't that she never had the chance but she was always too afraid to try it and was never with someone that she trusted enough to venture down that path. She always wondered why so many men are interested in anal sex. What is it about the back door that intrigues them so much? But she also knew she trusted him and that he would make it an enjoyable experience.

She also knew he wasn't going to give up, this was something he wanted to do, and she wanted it too, so she had to tell him. He had taken her out to dinner one night and when they got to the car, she took a deep breath and told him she had something important to tell him. Poor guy was worried that this was serious news. She scooted over in the car, kissed him tenderly, and told him that she wanted to give him her ass and that he would be the first man to ever enter there. She asked him to help her prepare, at that point he turned to her and kissed her deeply. "Baby, I didn't know you had never had anal sex before. I will be so very gentle with you my love. You will enjoy this, I promise".

Her body filled with excitement and fear at the same time and she threw her arms around his neck and held him close as she whispered in his ear to take her home. She scooted back to her side of the car and fastened her seatbelt. As they headed down the road she asked him for a favor. She said; "babe, when we get home, will you stand behind me, press against my body with our clothes on, and explain to me how you will prepare me for our magical moment when you take my virgin ass?" Without any thought he agreed.

They arrived home and started kissing before they even had their coats off. They got their coats off without releasing that kiss and just let them fall to the floor. He remembered what she wanted so he turned her around and pressed himself firmly against her back. He put his hands on her hips and he leaned down to her ear as began to explain what he would do to make her comfortable as he took her virgin ass and made it his.

He moved his hands from her hips and wrapped them around her waist. Gently massaging from her stomach on up to cup her breasts and then back down. His hands began to massage her nicely shaped buttock as he said; "Baby, I will massage your beautiful ass and you will begin to relax for me. My hand will move to spread your cheeks so I can rub my finger across you sweet, tight, ass hole". He did the motion as if to spread her cheeks with as much reality as he could with her slacks on. At that moment she began to bend a little and pressed herself back against him. "Yes, baby, that's right. Bend over for me. I will put just a little lube on my finger and I will circle the rim of that virgin hole. Oh, baby, you will feel my finger enter slightly. Take a deep breath honey, allow yourself to relax." He began to press his finger towards her anus through her slacks. The he pressed his thumb against her sweet hole and his fingers reached down and massaged her pussy. He pressed his back against hers somewhat forcing her into a more bent over position. Her body was reacting to his touch and his voice. Her hips starting to rock as if it was natural for her. "Baby, I will gently slide one finger inside your tight ass. After my finger has relaxed your ass I will gently ease in another finger and stroke your inner walls. When I have that hole ready for me to enter I will give your ass a loving spank and I will spread your cheeks (she takes a deep breath and begins to pant with desire)." My hand spreading your cheeks, the other hand guiding my hard cock towards that beautiful ass. I will align just the tip at the opening and press lightly. Oh, baby, you will feel the tip of my cock begin to enter, my hands holding your hips to maintain alignment. Feel that head press on and the tightness of that virgin ass as it becomes mine. I will massage your lower back. Baby, take a deep breath as the rim of my cock finally enters. I know I will moan with desire at that moment. I will be watching as my shaft enters you. I will stop if you want me to. Hold on baby, feel every inch inside your tight ass. I'll slap your ass while I enter you and that will be a part of the pleasure and part of the pain. I'm sure you will relax and enjoy to the point that you will back up to push more of me into you. Baby, you will feel my cock throb as the warm cum is released inside you". He then pushed his body firmly against hers and wrapped his arms around her again and began to kiss her neck and told her how much he loves her.

She could feel how hard he was as she pressed back. She made a quick more and turned around. She took his face in her hands, looked him in the eyes and with labored breathing she asked him to take her ass tonight. Show me my love; I want to know the joy you talk about. Take me on the journey.

He kissed her deeply, his hands massaging her back as he hugs her. He takes her hand and leads her to the bedroom. He undresses her, kissing her skin as it is exposed. He laid her on the bed then he quickly removed his clothes and joined her on the bed. He started at her ankles and kissed his way up her legs. As he passed her knees her legs instantly spread apart. She was ready; she wanted him to take her.

She sat up and placed her hands on his head and gently pulled him up. She looked him in his eyes and with passion she told him to take her. She was ready to give him her virgin ass and he had already gotten her to the point where she is ready, no more foreplay is needed for her at this time.

He put his hands on her hips and rolled her over so he could get her sweet ass ready to accept his now thick and throbbing shaft. Her legs seemed to spread naturally as he pulled her ass up in the air. He bent over and kissed her ass then began to rub that beautiful rump. He gave her ass a light slap and she responded with a very positive "oh, YES". She knew this was the beginning and she wanted this badly. She couldn't remember when she ever wanted anything as badly as she wanted this right now.

He turned his attention to her sweet ass giving her another light slap. His hand went down between her legs and his fingers grazed over her warm, wet, honey pot. He dipped his first two fingers inside to get them wet with her sweet and smooth juices. He then slid up between her ass cheeks and as he gently pulled her cheeks apart he bent over and licked that virgin hole. She didn't remember him telling her about that move but she sure liked how it felt. As his tongue started to circle her hole she began to rock back and forth. "Oh, baby, that feels incredible. Yes, yes, oh baby" she let him know how much she liked this surprise. The warmth of his tongue, the way he gently grabbed her ass cheeks to spread them apart. Then, without warning, he gave her two quick slaps on her ass.

Now that his tongue has moistened the area he moved his index finger in to circle the rim of that virgin ass. Pressing lightly at first and then finally pressing his index finger into her ass. She let out a moan that was obviously one of pleasure. He worked that finger around the inner wall to gently stretch that virgin ass. It was much tighter than he was prepared for but he gently worked it until she was relaxed enough to allow his second finger in. With his other hand he opened the lube and squirted a small amount on his finger that was now gliding in and out of her ass. His second finger slid in with ease. His fingers began to massage the inner walls of her ass. Going in deeper with each thrust. She started to rock back and forth just a little bit. He was watching her body and she was really rocking back and forth. He was pleased that she wanted it so badly. It made his cock even harder seeing the way her body reacted. She moaned with pleasure the entire time. She wanted this.

He leans over her slightly and with his other hand he reaches around and massages her breast. "Oh, baby, you feel so good. Are you ready to feel my cock inside you?" He asked. She didn't even take time to think about the question as she responded with a quick, "oh, yes baby, and let me feel you inside me. Take this virgin ass and make it yours".

He slowly removed his fingers from her now relaxed ass hole. He stroked his cock a few times to spread the lube from the tip to the base. Then he applied a little lube on the rim of her hole. She remembered to take a deep relaxing breath as she felt the tip of his shaft at her opening. This was it, she was about to feel his cock deep inside her ass. He pressed the tip in slowly. He watched as his cock began to enter her, as her hole wrapped around his cock. The head entering slowly and just as the well-defined rim was at the edge he slapped her ass firmly and then gave his cock one firm push to get that ridge past her opening. He let out a loud moan as her ass hole grabbed onto his cock. She moaned a deep guttural moan of pleasure. He started to rock slowly just inching his shaft in. In just a little then back just a little, slowly he allowed her ass time to get used to his shaft. His hands firmly placed on her hips so he could control the depth and speed.

She started to push back harder wanting his cock in deeper. He could tell that she really was enjoying this and that assured him it was ok to speed up and move to her pace. Her body began to shake as her orgasm hit. Her pussy was pulsing as his cock entered her. The cum, as it was released, began to drip down her leg and the room began to smell like sex. He start to enter her a little faster, a little deeper. Her ass is so warm and tight. After moving back and forth for a couple minutes his thrusts became deeper and he began to moan with each thrust. She was thrusting back forcing him to put every inch inside of her. She moaned her pleasure.

The feeling of her own warm cum dripping down her leg made her curious. She slid her hand between her legs, first just taking two fingers across her warm pussy to gather the juices and take it to her mouth to taste it. So sweet, so smooth, so warm. She took her hand back to that warmth and inserted one finger inside her pussy and she could feel the ridge of his cock pressed against the wall. Oh, yes, this was incredible; she just held her finger still so she could feel his cock gliding inside. She asked him to slow down for just a second, she had an idea. She could reach the top drawer of her night stand and she quickly grabbed her vibrating egg. "What are you doing?" he asked. She started to rock back and forth so he wouldn't stop completely. She built up the momentum again. She begged him; "slap me baby, don't stop fucking that ass, please don't stop. I want to feel that cock pulse as you fill my ass with cum. Don't stop fucking me".

Then he started to speak, "you like this hard cock in your ass baby? You want me to fill that ass up with my warm cum?" She didn't need to think about the answer because she was enjoying each and every thrust. Then the "dirty girl" came out in her and she replied with, "Yes, I want your hard fucking cock to start to throb in my ass. Fill me with your cum. Slap my ass baby; fuck me like you want it. Fuck that virgin ass like you mean it".

Then she did it. She put that vibrating egg on low and slid it just inside her vagina. In just enough that the vibration could be felt against his thick cock. His surprised was obvious as he blurted out, "what the fuck, damn baby, that is incredible. You are going to make me cum quickly now." He slapped her ass a couple of time and then grabbed those cheeks firmly.

Well, her change to the "dirty girl" was a turn on for him and he started to really fuck that sweet ass. He thrust his cock in harder, deeper, and faster. He slapped her ass several times leaving her cheek warm and red. She felt he was getting close so she pulled that vibrating egg out, she didn't want it to distract from her ability to feel the cum explode from his cock when his orgasm hit. One last deep thrust and she felt his shaft throb as his orgasm hit. At the same moment her body began to shake as the warm cum was released deep inside her. She reached between her legs and gently cupped his balls so she could feel them tighten as his orgasm was released. He moaned loudly as that cum filled her. He grabbed onto her hips more firmly as he thrust so deep inside her that his balls were pressed firmly against her dripping wet pussy. He let out a loud moan as his cum was released.

As his cock began to soften after his orgasm he slowly slid it out of her ass. He bent over and gave her ass cheek a nice kiss and asked her to stay right there and he would be back. He went to the bathroom and washed off his shaft then took a warm wash cloth to the bedroom where he gently wiped the cum and lube from her ass. He spread her cheeks apart and her hole was still wide open and she moaned lightly. He pulled the covers from the bed up and over her. He cuddled up next to her back. His arm wrapped around her with his hand cupping her breast. He whispered into her ear "I love you babe. Thank you for letting me take you on that journey. I do hope you enjoyed it. You were incredible my love, I enjoyed it." He kissed her neck and held her tight.

I won't lie, I am a little sore right now but it was wonderful."

He went on to say to her, "baby, that vibrating egg you surprised me with was something I would have never thought of and it was an incredible surprise. The dirty girl in you came out tonight and I really liked it. I hope you know that I will still want to make love to you in the more traditional way. We can save this for special nights." She didn't say a word but he knew she agreed because she squeezed his hand and held him close.

They fell asleep as he held her close. The next morning, while she was in the shower, he striped the sheets off the bed and got them into the washing machine. Later he dried them and re-made the bed. The entire time he had a smile on his face as he remembered the joys of his experience from the night before.

She was smiling in the shower thinking about the wonderful journey she was taken on the night before. There was no way for her to ever explain how happy she was that she finally let him take her virgin ass. She was hoping that he would show her that joy again but for right now her ass was a little sore, but it was pleasure pain to her. She would be reminded of that journey every time she sat down for the next 48 hours.

I HOPE YOU DANCE

She had left the party and was walking next door to a quiet pub. She was at the bar getting a drink when he come up behind her. He placed his left hand on her abdomen, his right hand cupping her left breast. He holds her tight and kisses her neck. "You look beautiful tonight. I can't stop thinking about you". He turns her around, kisses her softly and dances slowly even though there was no music playing.

She was enjoying the dance and held him close. They have been friends for a long time but they had never kissed before. She was very surprised by the kiss but she liked it all the same.

Ma'am . . . Ma'am . . . She turned to see the bartender holding her drink. She broke away from the dance to pay for her drink and she asked her friend if he would like a drink but he said he was fine.

With her drink in her hand he took her other hand and walked with her to a booth in the corner. They scooted into the corner of the booth. He put his left arm around her shoulders and laid his right hand on her leg. He kissed her cheek and said; "I want to hold you when you are feeling alone, comfort you when you are scared, and be there for you in the good times and the bad."

She laid her head on his shoulder and reminded him that he would have that chance. He needed to be patient. She was still recovering from a bad relationship and was having trouble being able to trust again. She was committed to him and had no plans to be with anyone else and he assured her he felt the same. "Hold me now", she said to him. "Let's spend some time building our friendship and see where that leads us".

She sips on her drink and they cuddled in that dimly lit corner booth. Her heart beating strongly. She knew she was very lucky to have him as her friend. He was so happy that she wanted to build on their friendship and he knew he could help her trust again.

He asked her if she would like to go to her place and cuddle on the sofa. She finished her drink and they headed to her place.

She opened the door to her apartment and as the entered he seemed to take charge. With both hand he held her shoulders and pulled her close and kissed her with passion. His arms wrapped around her and one hand moved up and he placed it behind her head. She was overwhelmed by his sudden passion. She found herself kissing him back. Her hands roaming on his back and she was pulling him closer too. She was relaxing in his arms. She felt safe with him.

He moved his hands and placed them on the sides of her face. His passionate kiss turned into tender short kisses. He stopped the kisses and he held her close as he said; "you mean the world to me baby. I wanted to kiss you sooner and now that I have tasted your kisses I am going to want more."

Their relationship changed that day and their kisses turned into so much more.

MORNING WAKE UP

I woke up this morning after an evening of strange dreams. I stretched my legs, spreading them to each corner. My arms reaching above my head as my body arched to stretch everything to prepare for a new day.

My left hand started to lightly massage my stomach, then my right hand. I began to extending my fingers to amplify the pressure. Rubbing and massaging in a kneading motion. I moved side to side, inching down lower but stopping before reaching the hair line of that moist box. Then I began moving up towards the breast. My body started to react to my own touch.

I then moved my hands to my breasts. Massaging each breast then moving towards the nipples. The areole very smooth at first but as the nipple firms up the area around it becomes rough. I teased the nipple by running my finger around the areole and my breathing became heavy. I began to tease my nipples more by pinching and pulling on them. Massaging the breast and pinching the nipples at the same time.

At that point, my legs spread wide inviting action to the warm wet center. My right hand reaches down and gently spread my full lips as my finger slid between them to feel the firm clit. As my finger touched it I could feel the sensation deep inside. I didn't waste time and just began to lightly pinch that firming clit and massage it in a circular fashion.

The entire time I continued to pinch my nipples, tugging on them. My body started to arch with desire, I was getting closer to releasing, the breathing very labored. Thumb now massaging my clit and two fingers slid inside my warm wet vagina. Slowly I started to pump those fingers in and out then increased the speed pumping faster. Nipples being pulled harder as I began pinching with slightly more pressure. Oh, yes, the orgasm is building, I want to release. A moan was heard when I curled into a ball as the orgasm hit. My vagina pulsing and grabbing my fingers that were now deep inside as the orgasm released creamy cum. I moaned out "oh, yes, yes, yeeeessssss". My fingers coated in white cum, my muscles started to relax. I put my fingers into my mouth. The cum coated fingers so smooth, the flavor so sweet. I licked them clean then laid there naked allowing my body to relax and for the muscles to calm before I went to the shower to clean up.

THEY MEET

He arrives at her place. He knows that he is going to feel the warmth of her body and the wetness between her legs. He knocks; she opens the door and is wearing a sexy black teddy with fishnet stockings. He enters and shuts the door behind him; she briefly looks into his eye but quickly lowers her eyes. She is holding the collar in her hands hoping her King will put it on her.

He reaches out, takes the collar and asks her to look into his eyes as he fastens the collar around her neck. He puts his finger thru the ring, gives it a light downward tug and he leans over and kisses the top of her head. He turns her around and gives her has a firm slap. Then he says; "Very nice my pet, this will be enjoyable for both of us".

He pulls her towards the bedroom, her breathing becomes heavy. The riding crop, feather stick, butt plug, and a couple vibrators are on the night stand. He has started to pat her ass cheek beginning to explore the area. "Permission to speak, Sir", she said lightly. "What do you have to say?" he asks.

"Please let me remove your shirt and suck on your nipples so I can show you my loyalty". He pulls upwardly in the ring and grabs her face. She opens her eyes to see him smiling at her. "You know what I like, make it happen". She removed his shirt and laid it neatly at the foot of the bed. Pulled his t-shirt over his head and laid it by the dress shirt. His nipples in front of her face and she wasted no time sucking that nipple into her warm mouth. One hand on his back, the other massaging and tugging lightly on the other nipple. He steps back and sits on the edge of the bed. He grabs her shoulders and pulls her down with him. "Please, Sir, allow me to remove your pants and let me see that firm cock". Permission was granted and she removed the rest of his clothes laying them down with his shirt. As she pulled his briefs down and his hard shaft appeared she gasped loudly. She wasn't thinking when she held the shaft in her hand, opened her mouth and took the head of his shaft into her mouth. He quickly grabbed her hair and pulled her mouth off of his cock and firmly spoke . . . "Did I give you permission to suck my cock?" He did not let go of her hair but pulled even more firmly on it keeping her head at an angle so she could even see his shaft. He slapped her face with his shaft. He knew how badly she wanted it. "I am sorry sir, please forgive me, I beg you, please forgive me, I know I have done wrong." She begged for forgiveness, afraid he was going to get dressed and leave.

He bent her over the side of the bed, grabbed the crotch if her teddy and quickly unsnapped it, pulled it up baring her white ass. He grabbed the riding crop and gave her a quick, firm, smack. She wanted to let out a noise but knew better. He looked at her ass and saw the bright red mark left behind. He rubbed it to ease the pain. Then gave her one more. With each smack she raises her ass just slightly and even though he wanted to punish her, he couldn't resist any longer. He has wanted that pussy for a while and his cock was throbbing already. You see, with her legs spread and her ass in the air, he could smell the scent of her wetness, he could see it glisten as it ran down her leg. He grabs her hips and raises her onto the bed. His hard cock rubs between her juicy lips grazing over her clit. She gasps, her back arches, and she wants it now. With precision he presses his hard shaft allowing just the head to enter her. She tries to move back to force more into her. He slaps her ass and firmly instructs her to be still. Grabbing her hips, she can feel him taking a deep breath and he enters her slowly . . . inch by inch. When he is fully inside her he slaps her ass one more time and instructs her to move with him. A few thrusts in and he orders her to be still. He reaches for the small butt plug, spreads lube on the plug and on her tight ass hole. He slowly presses the plug into her ass and he can feel it press against his cock.

He holds the plug with his thumb as he thrusts fast into her. It didn't take long before he let out a very sexy moan, his cock deep inside her, his hands holding firmly in her hips and she feels him throb inside her. He fills her with cum. As he begins to pull out he instructs her to be still and to squeeze the muscles so the juices don't drip out, He crawls under her so his head is between her legs. He grabs her hips and instructs her to lower herself onto his mouth. As she starts to lower he instructs her to release the fluids . . . and a combination of her juices and is cum spills onto his face. She can tell by the moans that he is pleased. He pulls his mouth firmly against her pussy, licking up every drop.

He rolls her over and wipes his face between her breasts, pulls in the ring, looks into her eyes and says . . . "You have now been marked by my scent. Do not wash that off, get dressed for work and we will leave now." She got dressed; he removed the collar, kissed the top of her head and told her he was pleased.

SNOWY NIGHT

The morning was a beautiful winter day. Sun was bright; it was chilly but normal for this time of the year. The work day was fairly normal until about 10:00am when the unpredicted storm hit hard and fast. Inches of snow were accumulating fast and cancellations started to roll in. First the schools, then the local mall, it was becoming serious. Folks at the office were wondering if they should head home early.

Betsy was worried about the long drive she had and was trying to decide if she should just find a place to stay here in town instead of risking the drive. Isabelle wasn't about to have her friend risk the long drive and staying in a hotel seemed silly so she invited her to come stay with her.

Betsy, an average height, 35 year old, petite woman, accepted the invitation and then the announcement was made that the company was closing in 30 minutes. They started to pack up their things and headed to the parking lot to brush the snow off of their cars.

They both arrived at the apartment and spent some time to talk about their drive home. The roads were very slick and traffic was slow moving. Isabelle turned on the fire place and put lasagna in the oven that she had just made a couple days ago and had placed in the freezer.

Isabelle poured a glass of wine for each of them as they sat on the sofa. They spent some time chatting about work but quickly switched to talk about the fact that they are both single and both had been hurt very badly by the men in their lives. Both had suffered mental abuse and managed to find the strength to move on. Isabelle, a middle aged woman slightly overweight, had a husband that reminded her often she was too heavy. She was hoping to find a man that would lover her regardless of her weight. Betsy's husband had managed to convince her that she was no longer sexy, her inability to bear children made her less of a woman to him, they drank a couple more glasses of wine and then the lasagna was warm. Isabelle served up lasagna, fresh French bread, string green beans, and some sliced fresh peaches and apples. They enjoyed the meal, laughing and finished off that bottle of Red Ass Rhubarb Wine that was purchased during a trip to South Dakota.

Isabelle gathered the dishes and the two of them washed and dried the dishes. When they were finished, Betsy looked and her and thanked her from a great meal and told her that if she was a man she'd want to kiss her after such a great meal.

That was when it started. Neither of them having a lot of experience pleasing another woman but what was the harm in trying tonight.

Isabelle moved closer, put her hands on Betsy's face and kissed her with an open mouth and their tongues danced in each other's mouth. Well that felt very nice, "Betsy, are you sure you haven't done that before?" asked Isabelle. They both laughed at what they had just done.

The wine had started to have an effect on both women. Betsy asked; "do you want to experiment more?" Isabelle was quick to reply with a yes. Isabelle talked about the fact that her most sensitive spot is her nipples and it turned out that Betsy also found excitement when her nipples are touched. They were entering a world that they didn't know much about but they will make the best of it.

Isabelle didn't waste any time as she was the first to pull her shirt off, Betsy was quick to follow. Isabelle moved closer, wrapped her arms around Betsy and unhooked her bra, Betsy did the same to Isabelle. They continued to stay pressed together, knowing that when they pulled apart their breasts would be totally exposed. They kissed quickly, separated, and the bras fell to the floor. As if it was instinctive, they both reached for the other's breast and massaged them. Isabelle started at the base of Betsy' breast and massaged out to the nipple. Noticing the darkness if her areola and the thickness if her nipples. It was beautiful and as she massaged closer to her nipples she noticed how they became firmer. Betsy pressed both of Isabelle's breasts together and moved towards Isabelle's firm nipples. Betsy saw that Isabelle had very large nipples and as she blew air across her nipple it became firmer. Their breathing was heavy, both feeling the warm juices starting to build between their legs.

Isabelle reached down to unfasten Betsy's pants. Betsy did not hesitate and helped to get her slacks off. Then Isabelle's pants went down. They each took off their own panties. Isabelle pulled Betsy close, their naked bodies pressed together. Isabelle ran her fingers through Betsy's hair.

Then both of them began to explore each other's bodies with their hands. Isabelle bent over and sucked Betsy's nipple into her mouth. She sucked her nipple in as her tongue flicked across the tip of her firm nipple. She moved from the right breast to the left and playfully pinched Betsy's nipples. Betsy leaned her head back and moaned as Isabelle suckled her nipple, she giggled lightly as her nipples were pinched. She was amazed at the way Isabelle seemed to know just what to do to make her body shake. It was like she knew what she was doing. Betsy pleaded; "Isabelle, I want to make you feel as great as you are making me. Please lie down and let me suck on your nipples too."

They lay on the floor and Betsy thought they would lay with their heads as the same end. Isabelle has another idea. After Betsy lay down, Isabelle lay beside her but laid down in a way that both could suckle on each other's breast. Kind of like the well know "69" position but instead of their heads between the others legs. They both suckled in each other's breasts pulling nipples into each other's mouth.

Betsy surprised Isabelle when she reached down and started to press her finger into Isabelle's warm, wet center core. She slide her fingers between her outer lips and felt he love button. It was so wet with a silky smooth goodness. Isabelle moaned out her pleasure and she returned the gift by exploring Betsy's warm pussy. She felt her firm clit and flicked it lightly. Two of her fingers found their way into Betsy's warm, wet, honey pot. As her fingers probed slightly deeper with each thrust she pressed her thumb against Betsy's firm clit and rubbed in a circular motion.

They both used their fingers to explore the firmness of their clit, the smoothness of the juices that were flowing so freely. Isabelle begins to suckle stronger, she could feel her orgasm building, she couldn't believe that she was about to take her over the edge. The way Betsy's warm mouth felt wrapped around Isabelle's nipple was causing Isabelle's body to throb. She knew she was about to have an orgasm so she slid her body down Betsy's. She pushed on Betsy's hip to lay her on her back. Isabelle then rolled over and straddled Betsy's face so each could see, feel, smell, and taste those juices that have been created. As Isabelle pulled Betsy's external lips and exposed her tiny firm clit she let out a gasp and said: "oh, Betsy that is just beautiful. You glisten with moisture, you smell so good. I am glad that this is the first pussy my tongue will enjoy." And then she went down and her tongue side along the side of Betsy's clit, going around it and coming back up. She stopped shortly and flicked that firm clit with her tongue.

Betsy took her tongue straight to the wettest spot and licked up the juices, getting her face covered with Isabelle's juices. Both of them were enjoying this meal of pussy pressing their faces into each other. Their tongues darting in and out flicking the firm clit. Isabelle was moaning, almost a hum as she licked Betsy's juices. Betsy was about to release her orgasm when she pressed he face firmly between Isabelle's legs moaning loudly.

Isabelle pulled her head up and told Betsy she wanted to cum and asked if Betsy was close. She wanted them to cum together. Betsy replied that she was ready to cum and asked Isabelle to thrust her fingers inside her pussy. At that moment they both began to finger thrust each other. Both knew enough about pleasure that they rubbed the clit while thrusting their fingers in and out. Isabelle could feel Betsy's muscles grab into her fingers as her orgasm builds. Both reached hard orgasm at the same time. Loud moans were released; Isabelle's fingers were dripping in moisture as Betsy's orgasm was released. Betsy's fingers were also dripping with warm juices from Isabelle.

They turned around so they were face to face. They shared a kiss and laid there wrapped in each other's arms. This sure was a winter storm to remember.

SHE WAS HOME ALONE

She was home alone, nobody was planning on coming over so she was going to relax by the fireplace. She was surfing the web when she remembered a website she has viewed in the past where she could view adult video.

She found the site and started to search for a video that would make her body react. She started by watching a video about a man and a woman exploring each other's bodies. She found it a bit boring but also realized she enjoyed watching the woman as she sucked on his cock. She had always enjoyed feeling a man's shaft in her mouth so she would rewind and watch that portion often just to watch that man's cock get thick in her mouth. She was fascinated as she watched that woman slowly suck that shaft into her mouth, just the head at first. She watched as she stroked that shaft at the base and found it so sexy as she watched his shaft grow. She was able to take the tip all the way to the back of her throat. As it grew she started to gag as it went too deep.

Before she knew it she was pulling on her own nipples and could feel that the moisture between her legs was brewing. She started to massage her breasts more forcefully. Rubbing around the base of her breast and working her way out to the nipple. She tugged firmly on her nipples, pinching them with enough force that she gasped with pleasure.

She stood up and removed her pants. While standing there she spread her legs and rubbed her moist mound, grabbing it then massaging. Her body was enjoying her play time. She slid down onto the floor where she took her two middle fingers and started to thrust them into her warm, wet pussy. Her thumb massaged her clit and she continued to massage her breast with the other had.

Her eyes closed, her head tilted back as she manipulated that beautiful pussy. Stroking it closer to the edge and just before the orgasm hit she stopped thrusting her fingers in and out. She didn't want this to end too soon and she knew her body well enough to know how to reach that big orgasm that causes her entire body to react.

She pulled her fingers from that pussy and put them in her mouth. She moaned as she tasted her sweet goodness, licking her fingers clean.

At that point she decided to search for a video of anal sex. Something she had never experienced but she wanted to try. The video she watched was perfect. The man's shaft appeared to be of average size so it was a good start. She lay on her back, legs spread and in the air.

He seemed very kind as he grabbed some lube and squeezed some onto his fingertips. He pressed her legs towards her chest and pulled her cheeks apart and her hole looked tight. He rubbed that lube generously around her hole and then slowly started to press one finger slowly in. You could tell by the look on her face this was new to her. He slowly pressed his finger into her ass and then he slowly added a second finger to stretch that hole out. As she watched the movie she leaned to the side and began to play with her own ass just like the guy in the movie. She was feeling great pleasure in the way it felt. There was some pain but it really did feel good. She knew she was going to need to expand her toy collection so she could experience this more later. All she had was a small butt plug so she reached for it, added some lube, and slid it slowly into her anus. She took a deep breath as she inched that plug deep inside. It took a few minutes for her to get used to it. She didn't enjoy it at first but after a minute she closed her eyes and found it to be very erotic. She started to slide it in and out just a couple inches at a time. She felt her body start to react. She reached up and felt hat her nipples were very erect. Now she needed to decide to stop now or should she play longer and see if she could reach an orgasm with this plug in her ass or remove the plug and stroke her waiting clit to release the orgasm that is so close to exploding right now.

LEFT AT THE DOOR

As she walked toward the door to go to her apartment she saw something sitting outside her door. As she got closer all she could tell as that it was wrapped very nicely with a beautiful bow, it's not her birthday, not a holiday, she couldn't imagine what this was. She unlocked her door, picked up this large box and went into the apartment. With the box placed on the dining room table she took the attached card in her hand. With her hands shaking she pulled the card out from the envelope and read the instructions. "Tomorrow night you will come home and put on this outfit. Do not add anything, if it is not in the box you will not be wearing it. A driver will pick you up at 6:00pm. You have an appointment with Teri, your stylist, at 6:30. She has been paid and has instructions on how to style your hair. A make-up professional will also be there. The driver will wait until you are styled properly and he will deliver you to me as soon as you are done". She assumes this is from her King but the card was not signed.

She had to see what this outfit looked like, maybe that would give her an idea of who this was from and where he might be taking her. Let's see what is in this box; black, sleeveless leather dress that looks like it will be above the knees; nylons and garter belt; black lace bra, short black jacket; black leather boots; and in a velvet bag there were two gold hoop earrings, two opal earrings, and a beautiful long necklace that was a combination if gold and silver. The lack of panties makes her believe that this is a gift from the King. It was going to be difficult to concentrate at the office tomorrow, she was very excited about whatever tomorrow night may bring.

It was difficult not to think about what the evening had in store for her while she tried to work during the day. Her co-workers kept commenting about the fact that she had a smile on her face all day.

She was thinking about that beautiful soft leather dress she was going to be putting on. When the end of the day finally arrived she shut her computer down, gathered her things and left the building.

Upon arriving home there was a note on her door. She was so excited; the note confirmed the gifts were from her King. She was looking forward to showing him her appreciation.

She stated to undress as soon as she entered the door. She quickly got into the shower to freshen up, didn't have to style her hair since her King was sending her to her stylist. She was so tempted to put on a pair of panties but since there were none in the box she followed the instructions and didn't put any on. She slips on the garter belt and she wonders how he knew exactly what size to get. Then she gently pulls up the nylons, such a smooth feeling on her legs, just putting them on made her feels so very sexy. She pulls the black lace bra from the box and outs it on. Another perfect fit, the bra presses her breasts together giving her voluptuous cleavage. Now, hoping the dress fits as good as everything else she slips the dress on over her head. Her eyes closed as she pulls the dress down and zips the back. Slowly she opens her eyes and turns around to look into the mirror and a single tear falls forms and hits her cheek. She wipes it away so it doesn't hit the dress and she looks at herself in the mirror. The dress was a perfect fit. Low cut showing off her cleavage and the hem line shows off her shapely legs yet doesn't look slutty. She looks at the time and has to hurry to get the boots, jacket, and jewelry on. Just as she pulls on her second boot there is a knock at the door. This is it, her night is about to begin. As she takes a deep breath she opens the door and standing before her is a very handsome man wearing a tux. He extends his folded arm to her; she hooks her arms into his, steps out into the hallway, locks her door, and walks with this escort out the front door.

He opens the front door of her building, takes her hand as she steps out, and takes her arm again to lead her to the limo right out front. Her heart starts to race. He opens the door of the limo and as she turns to get in, she looks at the driver and thanks him for all he is doing to make her evening so wonderful.

The limo stopped, they had arrived at Terri's Studio, the driver opens her door and she slips one foot out, then the other and the driver took her hand to help her out of the car. He escorted her to Terri's office where the magic would happen. The mirrors had been covered, it was obvious that she was not going to see herself until everything was completed. Her hair was washed, dried, and styled but it wasn't styled with a flat iron like she normally used. She wanted to reach up to feel her hair but Terri stopped her and told her to just be patient. The make-up artist came in and applied the makeup. As the last stroke of mascara was added, Terri pulled the cover down from the mirrors and turned her chair around so she could see what had been done. She couldn't believe her eyes. Her normally bone straight hair was now filled with beautiful bouncing curls. Her completion was flawless making her look younger with a blue/grey eye shadow that shows off her beautiful blue eyes. All of that topped off with a red/burgundy lip gloss. She wanted to go see her King; she wanted to see the look on his face when he sees her looking like this for the first time. She thanked Terri and the make-up professional for all they had done.

The driver came back in, gasped when he saw her and he took her hand to escort her out to the limo. As they walked he quietly told her how beautiful she looked. She asked him where they were going next and he became silent. She wasn't going to get a hint, she was anxious the get to where ever they were going to go, anxious to see her King.

They started on the journey to the next designation. She was trying to imagine where they were by the directions the driver was turning. Then she just sat back, didn't worry about where they were going, she just enjoyed the ride. After several minutes the car came to a stop, her heart started to beat faster.

The door started to open and she slid to that side. Then she saw a hand reach into the car, she extended her hand and he held it firmly, massaging her hand with his thumb. She turned so her right leg was out of the car, then her left. He pulled slightly on her hand as she exited the car and stood up. He kissed her hand and then stood back to see his woman and all her beauty from head to toe. Her hair was amazing, the make-up perfectly done, those lips were very inviting, the dress showing enough cleavage to be sexy and it hugged her curves, and her legs were so shapely in those black boots. "My pet, you are beautiful as usual tonight. I am so glad you could join me" he said as he leaned towards her and then kissed her on her cheek. She looked into his eyes and replied; "Thank you, Sir, for all you have done for me. I hope I am given a chance to show you my appreciation".

He took her arm as they walked into his restaurant of choice, Blackstones. She was so surprised that they were meeting in public like this. Their relationship was kept a secret from everyone. As soon as they entered the restaurant they were greeted by one of his co-workers. Her

King didn't try to hide her but instead pulled her close and introduced her to Brett. Brett said he was happy to meet the lovely lady that he has been hearing so much about. She really wasn't sure what to think, hearing that her King has told others about her was a big surprise.

He had made reservations and they were seated at a booth kind of in the middle of the restaurant. The waitress asked if he would like some place more private for the meal and he replied. "No, Ma'am. I want everyone to see this beautiful woman that is with me tonight. We will have our time alone later." As she sat down in the booth, he opted to sit across from her so he could continue to enjoy her beauty. He knew what she liked so he had already ordered for her. A heavenly drink of Rum was delivered to her. As she took the first sip she commented on how incredible it was. He smiled and told her he contacted the bar on the pier in Cocoa Beach and got the recipe for the Mai Tiki Tai drink she so enjoyed when she was down there years ago.

He reached across the table and took her hand in his. He looked into her eyes and told her how much he had been looking forward to this evening and how happy he was that his co-worker was there to see how beautiful she is.

She smiled at him and told him how surprised she was that he had told anyone about her. Reminded him that she thought hat their relationship was very secret. Then went on to tell him how thrilled she is to be with him and able to be in public with him as a couple.

The food was delivered along with another drink for her. He had ordered their famous Mac-n-cheese and they split the meal. He ordered a plate of fresh fruit for her, he got the chips. He knew that she didn't eat much and also knew she would enjoy the fruit. She was still healing from a past relationship where she was told she needed to lose weight so she has to work very hard to get the proper nutrition because she really didn't like to eat now.

They enjoyed the meal. Every now and then he would grab a grape and feed it to her. He really was treating her like a queen tonight. She had eaten all she could possibly eat and he stood up to sit on her side of the booth. As he slid next to her he leaned toward her and kissed her with his had placed gently on her cheek. He knew that she always felt even more loved when he placed his hands on her face when they kissed. She enjoys the tender touches. He settled in next to her and rested his hand on her leg. He couldn't resist himself and even though they were not in a secluded corner he had to feel her skin. He slid his hand up her leg and she took a deep breath. "Oh, Sir, that feels wonderful. You won't find any panties in your way, there were none in the box you had delivered." He gently kissed her and replied, "My pet, you don't have to call me Sir. I want you to think of me as your lover, your best friend, tonight." He saw a tear in her eye and he knew she thought that he was no longer going to be his King so he quickly went on to say; "you will always be my Pet, and I will always be your King. But, tonight, here in public, you are my girlfriend and my lover. I love you." He sealed that statement with a very passionate kiss.

The bill was delivered and he promptly paid for it. He took her hand and they walked to the door hand in hand. She asked him where he parked and that was when she found out that he had taken a cab so they could travel back to her place in the limo. As they stepped outside, he put his arms around her and kissed her again. His hands went from her shoulders down to her waist, pulling her in close. Then the limo pulled up. The driver quickly came to the back and opened the door for them.

They got into the car; he closed the window between their seat and the driver. He couldn't keep his hands off of her any longer. Before the limo was even moving he had his hand firmly placed on her now moist mound between her legs. He didn't need to warm her up; he could tell she was ripe and ready. Her legs spread instantly and he quickly started to slide two fingers inside and thrust them in, slowly at first and then faster and faster. She started to moan lightly very quickly. Her hand moved down to rub his shaft through his dress slacks. She could tell he was so very hard. She took her other hand and slipped it between her legs alongside of his hand. She got her fingers wet and quickly took her fingers to his mouth. He began to lick and suck on her fingers. That move took him over the edge. He sat back, unbuttoned his slacks, slid them down and exposed his beautiful firm shaft. He didn't even give her time to wrap her lips around his smooth tip. He pulled her legs apart, pressed he knees against her chest and he made love to her with so much passion. Her orgasm hit fast, her muscles pulsed against his shaft and he thrust deep into her and let out the sexiest moan she had ever heard as he filled her with his seed. He collapsed on top of her and held her close.

He did allow her to lick him clean before he pulled his slacks back up. He used his fingers to scoop the thicker juices from between her legs and fed them to her. She pulled her dress back down; he pulled his pants back up just before the limo arrived at her place.

They went into her place and the romance continued. He wanted this night to be for her. He knew he has used her to satisfy his sexual needs and really wanted tonight to be about the things she really liked. He knew how she felt about being totally naked so he had dropped off a very sexy teddy that would cover her mid-section but was short and low cut so their sexual moments won't be thwarted. He pulled her close, kissed her while massaging her back. With his hands on her face, he looked into her eyes and said; "as much as I love you in this dress, please let me undress you. I have something different for you to wear in your bedroom". She couldn't believe he was asking for HER permission but she quickly gave him the ok to do as he wished.

He walked her backwards towards the sofa where he pushed the dress up so he could reach the garter belt that was holding up her nylons. He slowly slid his hands up the inside of her legs. Her breathing becomes labored. She isn't wearing panties and he can see her honey pot pulsing the closer he got to that precious garter belt. He so enjoyed seeing what his actions were doing to her. As he reached the garter belt he smoothly unhooked her nylons. He moved his way around each leg unhooking each clasp. He could tell she was getting close to an orgasm but he didn't want her to release too soon so right after he rolled her nylons off he knelt between her legs, out his arms around her waist and held her close. Giving her a chance to relax and hoped it would slow down her orgasm. She bent over and kissed his head and ran her fingers through his hair. He reached up and pulled her forward so he could unzip her dress. He extended his body and kissed her neck and whispered his love for her into her ear. She was so confused because he has never voiced his love before. She threw her arms around him and held him tight. He unzipped her dress, and then he stood up and put his arms under hers and lifted her to her feet. He asked her to walk with him to the bedroom. With her dress unzipped he was able to access her bra and unhooked it. He rubbed her bare back, her skin so soft and smooth. He started to pull her dress and bra off her shoulders. He kissed her skin as it became exposed. He slid her clothing down just past her ample breasts. Her nipples were large and firm. He held one breast in each hand pulling on her nipples with light force; she let out a pleasure moan as her head tilted back. Her hands moved to be on top of his as he massaged her breasts so he was unable to let go. She was enjoying his touch. Once again he could tell her orgasm was getting close and he wanted her to wait so he removed his hands from her breasts and stepped back slightly. He reached over and grabbed the Teddy he brought for her. He slid it over her head and she reached her arms up for him. Oh, he couldn't resist her nipple when it was right in front of him so he quickly wrapped his lips around her nipple and sucked like he was hoping to pull milk from her breast. He moaned seductively as he suckled her breasts. He always thought her beautiful breast were her best quality. Her dress and bra hit the floor and he continued to suckle. She wanted him, she wanted to feel his firm shaft, and she knew there had to be droplets of precum on his smooth tip.

She was about to release an orgasm as she let him know of her need to feel his naked body next to hers. He reluctantly released her nipple from between his lips. As he stepped back to unbutton his slacks he pulled the teddy down so she was covered. But, he did reach up and pull each breast out so he could suckle these sweet nipples as soon as he could.

She started to unbutton his shirt and unbuttoned his slacks before he had a chance to take care of it. She wanted to see that beautiful shaft. She pulled the shirt off and she went to her knees where she started to lower his slacks. He stepped out of his slacks and stood there wearing just his briefs. With her hands on his hips she pulled him closer to her as she moved her mouth closer and she took that shaft into her mouth, briefs and all. She reached for the waistband and started to lower his briefs. Using her hand to hold his stiff shaft down as she lowered his briefs, as soon as the briefs were down lower than his thick shaft she began to stroke him. With her hand at the base, she opened her mouth and licked the tip of his shaft. She wrapped her lips around the tip and began to suck it in slowly. He let out a very loud moan as she neared the base. His hands on her head, guiding her along his shaft pressing her deeper with each thrust down his shaft. He lightened up his grip so she could suck his shaft without his guidance, she knew what she was doing, and she didn't need his guidance.

Her hands cupped his testicles and after her tongue reached the tip of his shaft she quickly moved her mouth to those sweet testicles. Licking from the center down towards the base of his shaft. She pressed on his hips to direct him to sit on the edge of the bed. Oh, the perfect height, and she laid him back. She spread his legs and pressed the up towards his chest, just far enough that she could see his sweet anus exposed. He wasn't resisting so she kept moving forward. She went down and licked his opening, licking around that sweet hole and then up and around his jewels. She gently sucked his right testicle into her mouth and rolled it across her tongue ever so gently. At the same time her finger was circling his anus that she left moist from her licking there seconds ago. Her mouth left his jewels and her tongue stares to kick his shaft like a lollipop but her finger never stopped circling. He was surprised that he was really enjoying it and he let her know as he moaned out to her: "slowly slip your finger in my love. Let me know what it feels like. Make my ass yours my love". She gladly did as he asked. First she got her finger very wet and she concentrated on making this an enjoyable experience for him. She slowly entered just the tip of her finger and started to gently massage the inner wall of his anus with the tip of her finger. He seemed to be relaxed and enjoying it so she wrapped her lips around his shaft again taking the tip to the back of her throat as she pressed her finger deeper into his ass.

He started to rock a little in an effort to get more of her finger to go in deeper. Yes, he was enjoying this. Her lips massaging his shaft with each inch she goes down and she starts to massage his anus more firmly until he asks her to stop. She doesn't push it; she stopped but continued to stroke his shaft with her mouth. She moved her hand to his shaft and stroked it at the same time her mouth rode it.

Quickly, without warning, he grabbed her, pulled her onto the bed and rolled her over onto her back. His shaft is so hard and he wanted it deep inside her sweet pussy. He wasted no time preparing her; he just spread her lips open and slid his shaft deep inside her until his testicles slapped against her. She was warm and wet because she had several orgasms as she was sucking on his shaft. He started to thrust hard and fast. His hands on her hips to ensure depth. She screams out, "Fill me with your seed. Make that cock throb inside me and fill me up". He obliged and with one last thrust he released a guttural moan as he released. He collapsed on top of her and wrapped his arms around her. "I love you baby. I want you to be with me always"

HE IS NOT DONE YET

She waited patiently for his arrival. He had told her he wanted to have totally control, that she needed to give to him totally. She wasn't sure why he would say that because she has always done what he asked. Well, maybe there was one thing she tried to always keep covered. He has always accepted her totally and tells her she is beautiful. She, however, can't accept what she feels are her imperfections.

Oh, he's here. Her heart throbs with excitement. She really needed to feel his touch; she needed to feel his soft lips.

The door opens; she is standing there in her turquoise nighty with her collar in her hand. He comes in, places the collar around her neck, and kisses her softly. He pulls her close and lets her know he is pleased with the way she looks.

He grabs onto the ring in her collar and leads her to the bedroom. Again, he pulls her close but this time he passionately kisses her. He stops suddenly, lightly pushing her away as he instructs her to lie on the bed, on her back. She looked at him with question in her eyes. She was so enjoying the kisses, she wanted more. He gave her a stern look as he said: "you heard me bitch. Do as instructed NOW". She quickly crawled onto the bed and lay on her back. She knew she angered him with her delay. Her arms crossed over her abdomen as she waits to find out what he has planned.

As soon as he saw she was in place as instructed he went to the drawer where she kept her nylons and he grabbed a handful. He went to the bed, leaned over to kiss her cheek, and he took her left hand in his. He pulled her arm out, wrapped a nylon around her wrist and tied the other end to the nightstand. He kissed her gently and moved down and tied her left leg to the base of the bed. Moving around the bed and doing the same to her right leg, her right arm. Kissing her before tying each limb. Her heart was beating faster, she was not sure what he was going to do; he had never tied her up like this before.

He got up onto the bed and straddled her body. He leaned over and kissed her with passion. Then he sat up, massaged her breasts, sliding her nighty out of the way. Gently pinching each nipple, pulling on each nipple . . . Becoming more aggressive each time. Her chest raising and lowering, she was enjoying his touch.

"Tonight, my bitch, I am going to use your body for my pleasure. I will expose all of you so I can kiss every inch of your body" he said in a soft tone.

Her breathing changed. She started to panic. She began to struggle, tried to get her arms free. She screamed out; "NO, NO, Please Master, I beg you, do not remove my clothes. I don't want you to see all of me. PLEASE, Master, I beg you to not do this. I beg you to not do that to me. Please use me without undressing me. Oh, Master, I beg for your understanding." Tears filled her eyes and dripped down the sides of her face. His hands holding her down until she grew too tired to fight. He wiped the tears from the side of her face but when he leaned to kiss her she quickly turned her head to avoid those lips that she so loved.

With firmness he grabbed her face, turned her head, and kissed her firmly. She did not kiss him back. She as angry, he knew how she didn't want to have her mid-section exposed, she hadn't lost enough weight, she didn't like the way she looked. She wondered how someone that can kiss her with such passion could want to do this to her.

He knew this wasn't going to be easy, but he knew it needed to be done. When they were together she was always covering up and he wanted all of her . . . every inch.

"You are my slave, my bitch, don't forget your role" he said firmly. "You must know that I find you to be beautiful, and you will let me show you that tonight. At that point he cut the straps of her night gown and exposed her breasts totally. He wrapped his warm lips around her nipples, one at a time. They were very firm and reacted well to his touch. She was relaxing, had stopped struggling, and the tears had stopped. He massaged her firm and ample breasts and suckled on them like a new born baby.

He got up, stood in front of her as he took his clothes off. She wanted to touch him and she let him know she wanted to feel his cock. He teased her with his growing shaft and ran the tip across her face, down her neck, and then he pressed her breasts together and slid that now firm shaft between them. Her hips began to move methodically as if to indicate she wanted to have sex.

He reached over and grabbed the long stick with small beaded chains on the end. He would drag those chains from her left wrist, up her arm, across her arm pit, around her left breast, around the right breast, down her right arm, stopping at her right wrist then repeating the process.

With her face in his hands, he tells her to look at him. She opens her eyes and he reminds her that she is not to struggle, not to fight it, he wanted to see all of her. He grabbed her nightgown and started to pull. It started to rip between her breasts and he tore it slowly down her abdomen. She turned her head to the side and tears filled her eyes again, she wanted to be able to drape her hands across her stomach. Since she couldn't, she cried silently. He kissed every inch of her body as it was exposed, as the nightgown was torn away. He really loved her body and didn't care that she wasn't tiny like a model, he loved her. Sure, as her Master he called her his bitch, his slave, but he would do anything for this woman.

He took the stick with chains from her neck, down between her breasts, zigzag pattern across her stomach, and then down between her legs. Then he did the same pattern with kisses. She could feel his firm cock pressing against her body. For a moment she forgot she was exposed, she loved the texture of his shaft.

Kissing his way down towards her center, he first reached down to dip his finger into her warmth. As his finger entered her, he pressed his thumb against her firm clit and moved it in a circular motion. Her hips moving and she started to moan; "oh, Master, that is incredible. I want to cum, please, Master, may I release for you?" He took a breath and told her to wait, to let it build. Of course, she would comply but the way he massaged her clit wasn't going to make it easy. She was on the edge and wanted to cum hard.

He turned around, his cock in her face while he put his face between her legs. Without her hands, she was not able to manipulate his cock to direct it to her mouth. He knew that and was enjoying teasing her with it. Swinging it above her face, just out of her reach.

The smell of sex began to fill the room and he couldn't hold back any longer. He dove in between her legs, pressing his face between her swollen lips, his tongue reaching out and licking her firm clit. She let out a scream of joy as he grabbed her hips and he attacked her honey pot. He told her to release, to feed him her juices. At that moment she raised her hips, pressed against his face, her legs began to shake, her entire body pulsed as she released other orgasm. His face covered in her juices he turned around to kiss her so she could enjoy the flavor of her own juices. She kissed his lips and licked around his mouth to taste the juices she covered him with.

His cock now pressed between her legs as they kiss. She could feel it twitch, he too wanted to cum. But, with her so tied up she couldn't help.

He looked into her eyes and asked if she would behave and not struggle if he released her. She replied; "Master, I will not struggle, I belong to you, I will behave". He went to the foot of the bed and released her ankles. He took her legs in his hands and pressed them up against her chest. He sweet pussy totally exposed, glistening with her juices. His hard cock was able to slide in without direction as he began to slowly ride his bitch. Slowly thrusting then a little faster, a little harder. His jewels slapping against her with every thrust until they firm up as the cum builds and is about to be released. He really wanted to push her legs up farther and take her ass but she had been through enough. He continued to thrust harder and faster. As he neared orgasm he began to moan; "you like this cock deep inside you? I am going to fill you with my seed bitch". At that second her orgasm hit, her back arched, and he felt the muscles of her pussy pulsing, grabbing his cock. He grabs her hips, pushes in deeper and moans loudly as he releases deep inside her.

He pulls out and squeezes the last drop from his shaft to land between her breasts. He looked in her eyes and said; "I have marked you with my scent. Do not wipe that off". Then he put his cock into her mouth so she could lick it clean while he reminded her what a good bitch she is.

He released her wrists as he sat on her stomach as he said with firmness . . . ."Don't try to cover up. I am not done enjoying your body. Do not try to cover up because you will be punished. You must submit to my desires, you will learn or you will be punished." As soon as he rolled off of her stomach she instinctively took her hands down to try to cover up what she could.

He saw her actions and slapped her leg instantly so she knew he saw, she knew he was angry. Slowly she removed her hands so she was totally exposed again. He leaned over and kissed he abdomen. However, he won't forget what she did. She must learn to relax in front of him; she has to know he loves her just the way she is.

She would be punished for her actions, she will soon learn . . . .

FIRE AND ICE—MAYBE

He had a key to her place yet, when she came home from work, she was surprised to find him at her place. They didn't usually meet on Wednesdays so she was pleasantly surprised. He greeted her at the door with a sweet kiss then he put her collar around her neck. She took a deep breath, she knew he wasn't there as a friend, he was there as her Master.

He took her purse and set it on the floor. He then began to undress her. First unzipping her coat and sliding it off her shoulders and tossing it off to the side. She just realized that she was wearing pantyhose and they were against his rules. However, she did have the crutch cut out so he could still gain entrance if he wanted to. In her defense, Wednesday was supposed to be the one day she could do as she wishes and was not under his total control.

He put his arms around her and slowly unzipped her dress. He slowly slid the dress off her shoulders, kissing her skin as it was exposed. As the dress continues to slide down, he kisses down her stomach and then he sees it—she is wearing pantyhose. He took a deep breath and let out a sigh. He just stood there looking at her. He looked disappointed and it broke her heart. With a voice filled with fear and on the verge of tears she says; "Master, I am so sorry, Sir. Please understand that today is Wednesday and I did not think you would contact me today. Before you get angry, I beg you to slide your hand between my legs, please Master, and slide your hand towards the honey pot. I beg you to trust me. Please, Master, I belong to you; I don't want you angry with me".

He quickly grabbed her hair and pulled it firmly. Her head now pulled back and she is looking at the ceiling, her neck is totally exposed. With a very firm tone he replied; "you better hope I am pleased my pet. I don't want to have to punish you tonight." Then he bent over and gave her neck a light bite. His hand reaches between her legs and slowly slides his hand up her inner thigh. As his hand reaches the center he feels the warmth and moisture, his fingers seem to automatically slide between her outer lips and enter the warm wet center. "Oh, my bitch, you have made me a very happy Master tonight" he said and he gives her a passionate kiss while his fingers continue to probe that sweet pussy.

Her body starts to grind onto his hand. His finger glides in and out of her warm wet pussy. With his other hand he unhooked her bra so he could get her big nipple into his mouth. Once the bra is removed he suckles her breast. Sucking each nipple into his mouth, one at a time, giving her a playful nibble every now and then. The room fills with the sound of her joy and the scent of sex. His fingers continue to thrust in and out.

She was now in front of him only wearing her crotchless pantyhose. He realizes that she is not trying to cover herself up. She has finally let go of her insecurities, she trusts him totally and knows he accepts her the way she is. He was so very proud of her at that moment. He held her face in his hands and kissed her like he couldn't live without her. He held her close and whispered into her ear to help him get his clothes off; he wanted to make love to her. His original plan was to have an evening of "Fire and Ice" but his plans changed and he was rethinking that thought.

She started to unbutton his shirt but he was anxious so he just grabbed his shirt and pulled it, popping each button off, tearing the shirt. He announced; "I want you my pet, I need to get my cock into that warm, wet, pussy". He then proceeded to pull his own pants off quickly and instructed her to get on the floor, on her back. He had put a blanket in the floor before she came home so she knew exactly where to go. Before she lay down, she put her hands on the waistband of her panty hose. "No, no, leave them on for now", he instructed.

He grabbed her ankles and spread her legs apart. He just looked at how beautiful her pussyfoot looked, those swollen outer lips wet with her juices framed by the opening in the crotch if her pantyhose. He moved closer, with his hard shaft in his hand he took that smooth mushroom shaped head, pressed past her outer lips and began to rub it across her swollen clit. She let out a gasp of joy, her hips started to rock slightly. With one hand he held the outer lips apart so he could see her clit react to the touch of his shaft. He slid that smooth head across her clit, slowly at first and then very fast. He watched as her lips became firm and swollen as her orgasm started to build. Without warning he trusted his hard cock deep inside of her in one swift move. She let out a scream of joy, moaning out praises to her Master. He grabbed her hips and thrust deep, hard, and fast. Moaning with each thrust, faster and harder than before. His jewels slapping against her with each thrust until they became firm. He dug into her hips with his fingers; thrust his cock deep inside her one last time. Her orgasm hit and her inner walls started to pulse and grab onto his throbbing cock as the two of them came together. His entire body went limp as he lay on top of her, kissed her neck gently. He sweetly said to her, "My pet, that was incredible. I was going to have an evening of Fire and Ice for you tonight; we will do that another time". He rolled off of her but never stopped holding her. As he lay by her side he continued to hold her close.

She started to move and he pulled her back and asked her not to go anywhere. She explained she wanted to get a warm cloth to clean him off. He just pulled her close and asked her to lay with him. He reached over and released her collar. He kissed her neck and snuggling next to her. They fell asleep on the floor, in front of the fireplace, in each other's arms. She never tried to cover herself up that night, she exposed herself completely to him and he was so pleased.

Fire and Ice will happen another day.

BLUE DRESS

She went to the store after work and she saw her Master. He saw her. Her nipples became firm when she saw him and he could see them pressed against her blue dress. He walked towards her, their eyes fixed on each other. The closer he got to her, the bigger the smile on her face became.

He reached out for her hand and she extended her hand to him. He pulled her close, told her how great she looked, and instructed her to go straight home after checking out. He made it clear to her that he wanted to have her tonight and he did not want her to change clothes.

She quickly got to the check-out, loaded her groceries into the car and went home. He was waiting for her and treated her with a kiss. He took her hand and led her to the tall chair by the kitchen counter. He sat in the chair, he had removed his shirt and she began suckling on his right nipple. At the same time; she was massaging, flicking, and teasing his left nipple.

He moaned with pleasure as she suckled. His hand grabs her hair and pulls it slightly. Not enough to pull her off his nipple but in a way she knew he was pleased with her actions.

As he reached for her breast he started to massage the top of her breast. She really wanted her nipples touched so she reached down and pulled her breast out so he could access it easily. He quickly started to pull on her nipple. She was now moaning as she sucked on his nipple.

He grabbed her hair firmly and pulled, forcing her off of his nipple. He reached down to pull his already firm cock out of his pants. She leaned towards it but he announced to look but not touch. With his cock in his hand and his other hand directing her head he gave her permission to lick the precum from the tip. She quickly licked the tip but couldn't resist wrapping her lips around that glistening tip. That caused her to grab her hair tightly and pull her head back. "Don't do that again", he said very firmly as he gave her hair a very firm tug. Then he simply pointed to his nipple and she knew she needed to get back to sucking. Yeah, he did enjoy having his nipple sucked and she didn't mind because she loved the way his nipple felt in her mouth.

As she was sucking he reached down and slid his hand up her inner thigh. She took a deep breath the closer he got to her core, she sucked harder and faster which was the response he was looking for. He let her know he was going to finger fuck that warm wet pussy. His fingers thrusting in and out, then his thumb rubbed her clit. That was when she lost it. She let out a loud moan of pleasure. He quickly put his hand on the back of her head and he was angry. "My finger fucking distracts you. I have not told you to stop sucking my tit . . . Get back to your duties . . . NOW". She went back to sucking and did not allow his finger fucking to distract her. He could tell by the intensity of her sucking every time she had an orgasm, and there were plenty.

He pulled her off the chair and ordered her to her knees. She reached up and out her hands on his hips as she opened her mouth. He grabbed her wrists and instructed her to out her hands behind her back. She let out a sigh, she wanted to get that hard shaft in her mouth, she wanted to feel the tip hit the back if her throat. She leaned forward and took his cock in her mouth and she quickly started to ride that thick shaft.

"Wait, be still, open that mouth wide and take the entire cock in your mouth. Open wide". She heard his instructions and did as she was told but she preferred to control the depth. He held her head firm, her hands behind her back. The velvet tip hitting the back of her throat and then he pushed a little too far, she almost gagged. Her hands quickly came from behind her back and grabbed his hips. He gave his shaft one more thrust and his shaft expanded as he released his load. The sounds of his pleasure moans filled the room. She swallowed every last drop that he gave her and licked him clean. He tucked that beautiful cock back into his pants and pulled her up to her feet.

She looked into his eyes and thanked him for taking such good care of her. He pulled her close and held her tightly. He kissed the top of her head, turned her to the side, slapped her sweet ass and thanked her for taking such good care of him.

WAXING

She had received her instructions and was ready to start her day. She put her nipple clamps on as she got dressed. As she firmed them up she gave the chain a light pull to make sure they were properly attached. She pulled on the sweater he left with her instructions and a pair of black slacks. A quick look in the mirror and off to work she went.

Imagine her surprise when she got to the office and saw flowers on her desk. The note read, 'tonight you belong to me'. She spent the day with a smile on her face. However, she felt it at that moment. You see, her body reacted to the flowers from her Master and her nipples became swollen and firm with desire. The clamps were on fairly tight and with the swollen nipples it was almost painful but it was a type of pleasure pain.

She had a meeting in an hour so she began to prep for that. 15 minutes before her meeting she received a text message from her Master instructing her remember to remove her clamps every hour, massage her breasts, and applying ice to her nipples to prevent them from getting sore. Her nipples are very sensitive and he didn't want her to lose the sensitivity he had grown to enjoy.

She instantly acknowledged his text so he knew she would follow the instructions. The anticipation of what he had planned had her so excited.

The day went fast, she left work on time and went straight home. He was there waiting for her with her collar in his hands. He quickly secured it around her neck, kissed her with passion and pulled her into the bedroom.

The room was glowing with the flicker of candles. On the nightstand was a bucket of ice. She smiled as she realized that tonight was going to be 'Fire and Ice'. She didn't realize that he became a firm Master at that moment, no more gentle kisses, and no more sweet words tonight. She will feel his full strength tonight.

He instructed her to strip naked in front of him. She hadn't seen him like this before but she did like to see him use his power. She removed her slacks first and didn't waste too much time as she pulled her sweater up over her head. She wanted to feel his touch and she knew the sooner she was naked, the sooner she would feel his touch. She stood before him wearing her black leather bra and black thong panties. She turned her back to her Master as she began to remove her panties so when she bent over he would have full view of her center core. He will be able to see that her pussy was glistening with moisture for him. He took a step towards her and gave her sweet ass a firm slap leaving a nice red hand print. She quickly rubbed her own ass in an attempt to ease the pain. She then reached back to unhook her bra. As her bra hit the floor, her Master smiled as he saw her standing there wearing nothing but her firmly attached nipple clamps.

He reached out, grabbed the chain that connected her nipples and gave it a firm tug. She let out a bit of a scream and took a deep breath. Her breathing became heavy at that point. He could see her breasts raise and lower with each breath. Now armed with a riding crop he gave her ass another slap and poked her and pointed to the bed. He instructed her to get on the bed, lying on her stomach. A couple more firm smacks on her ass with the riding crop but this time instantly rubbed with ice cubes to remove the sensation of the burn.

He grabbed a tapered candle and held it above her body with precision. Close enough she would feel the burn but far enough away it would not cause any damage to her skin. 4 drops of wax hit the small of her back. She gasped as each drop hit her skin. Then he followed that by rubbing an ice cube over those drops if wax.

She was surprised that the next series of wax drops didn't get the ice applied right away. That was because he was first pressing ice cubes against her tight anus. As the first sensation hit her hole she raised her ass in the air, letting out a scream. "Master, oh Master, I beg you ice the wax. Please, I can still feel the burn". He apologized to her. He was so enjoying the way her anus was reacting to the ice he couldn't stop looking at it. He massaged her ass and continued to watch as the ice cube melted between her cheeks and saw the water drip down and find its way between her legs going to her warm wet honey pot.

He rolled her over and dripped wax onto her abdomen and followed each drop with ice. With each drop if wax she would gasp loudly. With each touch of ice she would scream lightly. His wax drops headed lower, making its way to her pussy. He spread her legs apart and she quickly pressed them back together. She did not want that hot wax between her legs. He put the candle down and gave her pussyfoot a very firm series of slaps and he firmly said, "don't ever close your legs in front of me, Bitch. That pussy belongs to me. Open those legs and let me inspect MY pussy so I can see that you have taken care of it.

She instantly spread her legs and his hand took a firm grip, grabbing that sweet mound. At the same time he gave that chain between her nipples a very firm tug. He grabbed another ice cube and pressed it between her legs and instructed her to hold it there. At that moment he stood up and removed his pants and boxers. His shaft already hard.

He spread her legs wide and pressed his finger into her pussy. The ice cube had made it so very cold; he knew it was too cold for his cock to enter. He grabbed the tube of lube from the night stand and applied it to his cock and around her sweet tight hole. He took her legs in his hands and pressed her legs up towards her chin, her ass now in plain view. With his cock in his hand he presses the tip against her ass . . . She takes a deep breath as he presses the head in. Her moans almost a scream as he pushes a little further. He enters her slowly, pressing in a little and then pulling almost out, pressing in further each time. Just before he gets his entire share inside her he presses the small egg vibrator inside her pussy and turns the vibration in low. He can feel the sensation on his shaft as he enters her tight ass. He begins to let out moans if joy. Her hips start to move with him as she gets used to his entry. Her moans are filled with both the sounds of pleasure and pain. He asks her; Do you want my cum to fill your ass? You want to feel my load deep inside this tight ass?"

She quickly replies; "Yes, Master, Please release in my ass. <Her breathing is labored>. MASTER, Please let me cum with you. I beg you to let me release with you".

As he grabs her hips he screams out his request to her . . . "Now, NOW, cum now with . . . . MMMEEEEEE" as his body tightened and his load is released.

She felt his power that night. There was no doubt he owned her. He was her Master.

SURPRISE

It was a normal Saturday morning. Nothing planned for the day but some light cleaning and a day of relaxation. As she walked down the hall he can out of the bedroom behind her with a scarf in his hand. The next thing you know he has placed the scarf over her eyes, she let out a playful scream of surprise as she raised her hands to feel what he had just placed over her eyes. As he stood behind her he gently out his hands on top of hers as he pulled himself closer and kissed her gently on the nape of her neck.

He slowly moved his hands from her face and seductively slid them down to her shoulders, down her upper back, then under her arms resting firmly on her waist. He turned her around and firmly pressed his ops against hers. Pushing her against the wall and kissing her with such passion that she was overwhelmed. The two, so into that kiss that they wouldn't have noticed if anyone had walked in at that moment. He slides her along the wall towards the spare bedroom. When he reached the doorway he held her tightly and walked her backwards, still kissing her, until they reached the bed. He playfully tossed her on the bed; she is still blindfolded and smiling. Like two teenagers they rolled on the bed with their legs wrapped around each other. The room willed with moans of love and passion. She let out some giggles when he would give her a playful poke in the side. She enjoyed having the blindfold in so each move was a bit of a surprise. She totally trusted him so she had no fear at all. After rolling back and forth for a few minutes, he rolled her on her back and with one knee on each side of her waist he held her there, holding her hands down beside her head. He bent over and kissed her lips ever so softly, kissed her nose, and kissed each eyebrow before he released her hands.

He unzipped her sweatshirt exposing her beautiful perky breasts. He bent over kissing each nipple and then playfully sucking each one into his mouth. After he gets each nipple sufficiently wet he blows softly on it and turns that already firm nipple even harder. She giggles when he does it and he so enjoys seeing how her body reacts and arches for him with each chilling puff of air.

He pulls his T-shirt off and lays his naked chest against hers and kisses her some more. Their bodies pressed together and he wraps his arms around her body and slides her sweatshirt off. He loves the softness of her skin and the aroma of her body when she is ovulating. Yes, he notices the subtle differences in her body when she is releasing her eggs. He knows that when he makes his way between her legs the juices will be even sweeter during this time.

"Oh, baby, [he kissed her between her breasts], I want to make love to you [he kisses her just above her belly button], I want to plant my seed inside of you [he unbuttons and unzips her jeans and kisses just above her pussy], I want you to carry my baby." He then begins to slide here jeans off and removes her pretty purple panties. He gently removes the scarf that was being used to blindfold her as he says; "I want you to be able to see the man that will be the father of our baby as I make sweet love to you."

She watched as he removed his jeans and as he removed his briefs. Her breathing became heavy and she could feel the silky smooth juices flowing between her legs. She thought he was the sexiest man alive and felt so lucky to have him as her own. Neither one of them had a body that would be shown on the cover of a magazine but they loved each other regardless.

With love in her eyes she asked him to bring her that beautiful cock and let her feel the texture with her tongue. He crawled back on the bed and, with his cock in his hand, he teasingly slid the tip across her wanting lips leaving a small trail of precum for her to taste. Then he said to her; "baby, you have a way of making my cock pulse when it is inside your mouth and I want every last drop to be released deep inside your warm wet pussy today. I promise to feed you some protein later." Then he lay down next to her, wrapped his leg around her as he pulled her close so he could feel their naked bodies mold together. His hand glides down her body and slides between her legs. The silky moisture was abundant. He slips one finger inside at first followed by a second finger gently massaging the warm walls of her pussy while his thumb rubs sweetly on her tender clit. He know that when she if ovulating every inch of her pussy becomes even more sensitive to touch and he enjoyed watch her reach the peak just before her orgasm is released. He knows just when to stop before going too far. He worked that clit, massaged that pussy, and kissed her tender lips to the point that she was about to explode with excitement. He removed his fingers and held her close as he rolled on top of her. His firm along shaft slide between her legs and that smooth tip found its way to her opening. With his legs he pushed her legs apart and he looked down as his shaft started to enter her honey pot. Her hips raised as the head entered, she wanted it badly.

He legs wrapped around his hips in an attempt to force him in farther but he was really enjoying watching her reaction as he pushed in slowly, one inch in then almost out . . . Two inches in and almost out until his entire shaft was deep inside her and his testicles were pressed against her body. He began thrusting into her slowly at first but built up the speed fairly quickly. He grabbed her legs, pressed the, up towards her chest and thrusts harder and faster. She is moaning her love for him and he was moaning with each thrust.

As his release gets closer he grabs her hips and with one final thrust and a very loud moan he held his shaft deep inside her as it pulsed and twitched until the last drop if his seed was released inside her.

He lay on top of her, holding her close, allowing his shaft to shrink back down.

GOOD MORNING

As she sleeps on her stomach he wakes up and rolls closer. Pressing his body against her back, moving her hair to the side and kissing her neck. 'Good morning baby', she whispers as she moves her body back and closer to him,

His finger glides from her temple, down her face, along her side and then he wraps his arm around her and holds her tight against his body. 'Good morning baby' he whispers back. As she starts to wake he kisses her neck and asks her to relax. She is enjoying his touch so much that wasn't a problem.

He moves closer, she can feel his already firm shaft against her leg. She takes a deep breath as his hand glides down to her body. Her soft moans begin to fill the room as her body starts to squirm at his touch.

As his hand moves towards he warm center she rolls slightly to be partially on her back, only stopped because he was there, behind her. He moves slightly so she is completely on her back. As his hand goes directly to her warm center core, he kisses her and this tongues dance together.

Sounds of his moans begin to fill the room. He wants her badly; he wants to make love to her.

Her swollen breasts and firm nipples are in front of his eyes, he takes his hands and envelopes her firm breast, his mouth lowers, and he sucks her right nipple into his mouth. His tongue flicking across her nipple as he suckles. He massages her left breast and lightly flicks her stiff nipple. Her moans become very loud, he knows how to suck her nipple and make her juices flow.

She reaches down and gently takes his shaft into her hand. She glides the tip across her leg and can feel a tiny among of pre-cum against her skin. She begins to stoke he's shaft, starting at the base and slowly working towards the tip. At the tip she glides her thumb around the well-defined rim and then her fingers glide over the top before her hand glides back down that firm shaft massaging along the way. Once she arrives back at the base she starts back up towards the tip. Allowing her hand to grace over the tip before going back down. Her strokes pick up the pace that harder he sucks in her tit. More fluids spill out the tip. He pulls away before she manages to massage his shaft to an orgasm.

He rolls on top of her and looks into her eyes as he says: "I love you baby". He shaft, firm from her stroking, glides swiftly between her legs. He takes he legs and pushes them up against her chest. Her pussy shimmering with moisture, the tip of his shaft is right at her opening and he teases her just a little by pressing the tip in but going no further.

She starts to rock her hips trying to force his shaft to enter her. He laughs lightly at her attempts and found her antics to be somewhat amusing. He takes his shaft in his hand and rubbed the tip against her clit, up and down, slowly at first but then moving faster. He can't tease her any more, he is too close to an orgasm and he can't hold back any longer. The swiftly presses his entire shaft deep inside her pussy. She lets out a scream if pleasure. He trusts deep and continues to move in and out at a fairly fast pace. Her juices splattering with each thrust.

As they both reach orgasm at the same time and the sounds of their joy fills the room. Her body pulsing, her inner walls throbbing as she grabs his shaft to pull the last of his juices from him. As his cock throbs and his last drop is released his entire body relaxes and he releases her legs and he lays down on top if her allowing his cock to shrink. As his cock slipped out he rolls over and cuddles with her.

Two people so much in love. So beautiful.

FORGOTTEN TRAINING

I need to go to work extra early so I let you sleep in. But, after my shower I see you lay naked on the bed. I stood there and stared at the most wonderful Master, the sexiest Master, the man I belong to. I could hardly move because I was so touched that this man shared a bed with me. I felt so very lucky.

He sensed me being there and so sweetly asked what was wrong. I simply replied; "nothing Master, I see you there and the thought if leaving the house without pleasing you bothers me". He tapped the bed and said; "come here my pet, bring your vibrator, show me how you make that sweet pussy sing for me". I couldn't believe it. I quickly grabbed my vibrator, laid next to him with my feet at the head of the bed. I moved up so my face was near his growing cock. Vibrator humming and strategically places on that firming love button. I got that pussy to start to pulse and throb for my Master. I rolled slightly to the left and my lips grabbed onto his beautiful cock. As I lay on my side my right leg is raised so he could see that pulsing pussy. He grabbed the vibrator and continued to take me to the edge. I continued to suck his cock, my mouth riding up and down, from the tip to the base. I was moaning with pleasure, this pussy about to explode with sweet juices, juices that belong to him.

Then it happened . . . Smack . . . Smack . . . the crop finds my ass . . ."faster, harder bitch . . . Pull that cum out properly". I felt bad that I had not been doing as I had need taught. I sucked harder and faster than ever before. He took two fingers and fucked that pussy that belongs to him. He felt the walls tighten around his fingers. His cock started to twitch, he was about to feed me. I let out a loud moan as he fed me, at the same time my body arched as I coated his fingers with my love.

I cleaned him up properly, I got dressed, kissed him with passion and I left for the office. "Have a great day my pet", he said.

I was anxious to get home that night; I wanted the fire to continue to burn.

When I arrived home I was surprised that he was waiting for me. The riding crop was in his hand, my collar was on the table beside him, and a stern look was on his face. I sensed I was about to be retrained when he instructed me to strip naked in front of him. I wasted no time and did as instructed. He stood up and with the collar in his hand he walked towards me. He placed the collar around my neck then pulled my hands behind my back and tied them together. Then he hooked his finger through the large metal ring on the front. "You need to be taught the proper way to suck cock my pet. This morning you were having your fun without concern about my needs." I knew he was right, I had no reason to argue with him about this. I bowed my head as he lead me to where he was going to sit. I didn't like having my hands tied and a tear began to form. I worked hard to try to stop the tear from falling but without the ability to use my hands to wipe my eyes I couldn't stop it. I will just keep my head down and that should take care of it.

He tugged on the ring to instruct me to my knees. Once I was on my knees he tugged on the ring to force me to look up. As my head tilted up the tear fell down my cheek. He pointed to his zipper then he saw the tear. He reached down and wiped it away as he said; "my pet, you know I only do this so you behave better the next time. I love you with all of my heart, but you were not doing as you were taught earlier. Please don't cry, learn from this lesson and we will both enjoy this."

I smiled at him as I reached and unbuttoned his slacks and lowered the zipper. I pulled his pants down to his ankles then reach up to remove his boxer briefs. He was still flaccid which surprised me. I gently pulled his briefs down to expose his beautiful penis.

He took my head in his hands and tilted my head back so I could look into his face. "baby, I know how you like to feel a penis grow in your mouth. I am working so hard to keep this soft for you, I suggest you wrap your lips around it quickly. Seeing you naked and on your knees makes it very difficult to keep myself soft."

He sat in the chair and I inched myself over so I could bend over and suck his flaccid penis into my mouth. My tongue placed under his penis as I wrapped my lips around it at the base. It didn't take too long as I began to suck before he was starting to grow in my mouth. The way it felt as the shaft grew in my mouth. My mouth gliding up and down and with each stroke my tongue flicked across the tip. It didn't take long and his penis consumed my mouth and the tip was pressed against the back of my throat.

Knowing how I felt about my hands being tied, he reached down and untied them. I quickly moved them to the front so I could cup and massage his sack as my mouth sucked that now thick and long shaft. One hand massaging the sacks while the other gliding up the shaft with my mouth.

The tip was now swollen and the velvet skin at the time was very tight. The ridge was so very well defined as my tongue licked around the ridge. I could hear his light moans so I felt I was doing things properly. Then he began to rock his hips. He places his hands on my head holding it firmly as his shaft thrust in and out of my mouth. A couple of times he thrust in so hard and fast I had to pull back slightly as I gagged but I went right back to sucking as he continued to thrust in and out. I could feel the veins with my tongue, they are so well defined. I could feel that his sack was getting firmer and he was getting ready to fill my mouth. I started to suck with more determination at that point. Pushing that head deep into my throat so I could feel the velvet tip glide across the roof of my mouth, my tongue gliding along the underside. Flicking at the ridge before I opened my mouth and took it in deep again.

I felt his penis throb slightly, he was getting close. I massaged his sack lightly with the next stroke of my mouth around his penis. With his hands twisted in my hair he firmly grabbed my head and let out a loud moan. The pulsing became stronger as his orgasm hit and his cum was released deep into my mouth. I felt the first warm shot hit the back of my throat with force and the rest hitting the roof of my mouth and gliding down my throat. As the throbbing stopped I slowly pulled my mouth off of his shaft licking the tip in an effort to get every last drop into my mouth. Squeezing his shaft lightly pushing the rest out and I kissed that off the tip.

He tilted my head back as he leaned forward and kissed me with passion and said: "I love you my pet. You've done very well. Now clean me up properly and I will take you out for dinner."

REUNITED

They hadn't seen each other for over 20 years but when they reunited again all of those years seemed like yesterday. Sure, his hair was now gray and she had put on a few pounds but the attraction was still strong. They happen to find each other on-line and were quick to start e-mailing back and forth, texting, calling and then, finally, made plans to meet face-to-face.

She was so nervous. She was self-conscious about her weight but she really wanted to see him again. She was going to invite him to her place but thought that maybe some place more public would be a better idea.

They met at a local pub where they could get a bite to eat and maybe have a beer. When she arrived she was surprised to see him waiting for her at the door. Oh, my, this was it. He is incredibly handsome and she was hoping he still found her to be attractive. She went to open her car door and there he was. He saw her pull in and had run to her car to open the door. He held out his hand to help her get out of her car. Her heart fluttered with excitement. She stepped out, he never let go of her hand. As she stood up he was quick to out his arms around her and give her a nice warm hug. As he pulled her closer, he whispered into her ear something he used to say to her when they were in high school, "baby, you look wonderful tonight". She threw her arms around his neck and gave him a firm squeeze, "you remembered, how wonderful".

They released the hug; she turned to grab her purse from the car. When she closed the car door he took her hand and said, "I am not letting go of you again sweetie" and as they took a few steps he pulled her close so he could move his hand and wrap his arm around her waist. He is much taller than her. He bent down and kissed to top of her head. She looked up at him, pressed her hand on top of his at her waist, and smiled. She put her arm around his waist and hugged slightly.

At the door he reached out to open it and pressed on the small of her back so she could go in first. He took that opportunity to take a good look at her nice back side. He stood there, shaking his head back and forth and simply said, "nnniiiiiiicccee". She heard him, reached her hand around and grabbed his buttocks and gave it a playful squeeze.

The woman inside asked them if they wanted a table or a booth and at the same time they both replied "booth". Then they giggled like school kids when they realizes they said it at the same time. The hostess led them to a corner booth; she could tell they were going to need privacy. It was perfect. It was a rounded booth so they could scoot around and sit side-by-side.

They both took a few minutes to look at the menu. He was quick to place his hand in her leg and it didn't take long for him to start to rub her leg. He was still in love with her, yeah they both aged but his heart was still full of love for her.

The waitress came by to take their order. She knew she wouldn't be able to eat because her stomach was in knots with excitement. He was feeling the same but neither one wanted to say anything. He took a chance and told the waitress that they would split an order of cheese fries with ranch dressing in the side with a pitcher of Miller Lite. He handed the waitress the menus, looked at her and said, "I hope you don't mind that I ordered for us. I hope you still like cheese fries and Miller Beer sweetie. I remember we used to get this on almost every date." A single tear formed in her eye, she was so touched that he remembered. She let him know she approved by reaching for his face with her hand and kissing him softly.

He put his hand on her neck, reaching around to cup the back of her head and he kissed her with passion. His mouth opened as did hers and their tongues danced together just like they did years ago. They adjusted their bodies but never released their lips. They kissed like that for several minutes only stopping when they heard the waitress drop off the pitcher of beer and two glasses.

She was a bit embarrassed that they were caught in such a passionate kiss but it did feel so very good. He poured a beer for her and one for himself. He tapped his glass to hers and said, "Here's to reuniting and finding the passion again". She replied with a simple, "cheers", and a smile.

They settled back into their booth where they began to talk about what has happened over the years. They had shared much of that information via emails but now they could expand on that. They each bragged about their children and grandchildren. Showing pictures they had on their cell phones. But, every now and then he would lean over and kiss her randomly. Just a quick kiss but she loved his spontaneity.

The waitress brought their cheese fries. He poured each of them another glass of beer as he toasted to her a wish for a long renewed friendship filled with love and laughter.

They shared the cheese fries just as they did when they were in High School. Feeding each other a fry every now and then. There were giggles and smiles as they finished their appetizer and as she fed him the last fry he looked at her and asked if she would like to go somewhere more private. She felt comfortable with him and suggested they go back to her place.

He paid the bill and they headed out the door. He opened her car door for her, gave her a kiss, and said he would follow her.

They weren't too far away so it didn't take long to get there. They walked to the door and as she unlocked it he kissed her again right before she opened the door. As soon as they walked in and the door shut behind them he wasted no time at all. He took her in his arms and kissed her with firmness just like he did when they were younger. His hands roaming her body as he is kissing her. At one point his hand went Nader her shirt and his hand touched her back. Feeling his hand startled her a little and she quickly stepped back and pulled her shirt down. She lovingly looked into his eyes and said; "oh, sweetie, the body under this shirt is nothing like the body you last touches years ago. I am not as thin as I used to be". He put his finger against her lip as if to indicate shhhh and he said; "but, baby, I have aged too. But in the short time we've been together I know that I still have deep feelings for you just like I did so many years ago. Please let me touch you again but if you are not ready I will back off and wait until you are ready."

She tilted her head back, reached up and kissed him lightly and thanked him for understanding. She took his hand and slid it under her shirt and onto her back. She asked him to go slow. He pulled her close and massaged her lower back as they kissed. She could feel her body reacting to his touch and she could tell that she too still had deep feelings for him. Over the years since they last saw each other she had never found anyone that could kiss like him that could make her melt with desire like he does. They would have several more meetings in the near future. This friendship will continue on for years.

HELLO, CAN I STOP BY?

He didn't complain when he got the picture of her beautiful smiling face and thought this might be a good time to talk about how he felt about her beauty and see how she would react.

Her phone rang and the caller ID showed it was her friend. He didn't usually call; email was their main way of communication. However, she really likes hearing his voice so she quickly answered the call. She answered the phone with the standard "Hello".

He thanked her for the picture and told her how great she looked. She was glad he couldn't see her blush. Then he said; "I am going to say something. Can you promise that you won't get mad?"

She replied; "oh, my, I can't think of anything you could say that would make me mad. I promise that I won't get mad"

He took a deep breath before he said anything because he really wasn't sure he should move forward with his thoughts but he did it. "Your recent picture shows some nice cleavage and I'd really like a chance to kiss right there between your breasts"

"That would be very nice. I would like that." She replied.

Those were the words he was hoping to hear. He went on to ask; "how would you feel about me reaching down your shirt, pull out your right breast, and suckle on your nipple?"

She responded to his question by saying; "oh, my friend that would be wonderful. My nipple would like to feel your warm lips wrapped around it. Would you mind if I held your head as you suckle that nipple as it firms up while in your mouth?" She had hoped she didn't go too far but her body was starting to react to his voice, to his questions.

He decided to take it one step further by asking if she would like for him to expose both of her breasts and suckle on one while lightly pinching the other.

By now both of her nipples were hard and she was starting to massage both breasts. She assured him that she would enjoy it if he would do just that. She went on to tell him he should come see her someday and actually do the things he was talking about.

His reply was simply; "yes, we should do what we can to let this happen. I am sure I can make you smile".

Oh, no, an interruption. She asked him to hold on a second, someone was at the door and she had to answer it. She was so anxious to finish the phone conversation that she didn't even look into the peep hole to see who was at the door, she just opened it. There, on the other side of the door, with his phone held up to his mouth he smiled and said, "Hello, you busy? Sorry I didn't call first, can I come in?"

She pressed 'end call' on her phone, reached out and took his hand as she pulled him in so she could shut the door. She giggled when he came in and she joked with him about how sneaky if was to call with his ideas and to show up at the door like that. His response was simple, he wanted to call so if she didn't like the idea he wasn't going to knock on her door.

Even thou he said what he wanted to do and she indicated she would like that; they were both shy about making it happen.

"I see you have on the same shirt you were wearing in the picture. It looks even better in person." He said with a smile,

That was all she needed to hear to relax her. She took his hand and moved it near her breast. She reached in, pulled out her breast and lay it in his hand, "oh, my, your hand is a little cold. Perhaps you should wrap your hands around my breasts to warm them up before you start to play with those nipples."

He is taller than her so he put his arm around her and led her to the sofa to sit down. Then he knelt in front of her. While looking into her eyes he opened his mouth and wrapped his lips around her large nipple. She held his head as he suckled her nipple. He body was starting to react, her head tilting back, she began to moan lightly.

He reached over to expose the other breast and, without saying a word, he began to suckle. His lips around one nipple while he pinched and pulled lightly on the other. She loudly blurts out, "YES" as her body arches and her moans became louder. He was sucking like he knew what he was doing and he was going to build her to a strong orgasm quickly. She was massaging his head as her orgasm began to build.

He stops just long enough to tell her to please cum for him. He wanted her to release while he sucked on her nipples. He could tell her body was pulsing and close to releasing. She was so close it didn't take long before her fluids began to flow. Her pussy pulsing as the orgasm hits hard. Her body tightens up; he sucks harder, her body shakes with desire and then completely relaxes. He knows he has taken her to that orgasm. He pressed his head between her breasts. She held his head and told him how that felt incredible.

He looked up at her, gave her a quick kiss, and said; "let's sit here for a while so your body has a chance to recover".

She replied by saying; "that was incredible. I would like the opportunity to bring you to an orgasm just as strong." He sat in the sofa, out his arm around her and held her close. "I sure am glad you didn't get mad. You are a special friend now."

He surprised her often and they enjoyed exploring each other. They always had their e-mail conversations but would enjoy other fun now and then. They would find ways to sneak in some nipple suckling and eventually he allowed her to remove his pants so she could suck on him. He soon discovered that she enjoyed feeling him inside her mouth. She enjoyed feeling his veins bulge for her when he became fully aroused then the feeling of his warm cum hitting the back of her throat.

She was glad he stopped by that day and looked forward to the next surprise visit from him.

THE OTHER WOMAN

He had mentioned before how much he would like to see her with another woman and tonight was going to be that night. She went home early to get things set up so when he arrived all of the little details were taken care of.

He walked in and found her sitting on the sofa with a female friend. She stood up, hugged him with passion, kissed him deeply and told him that she would like to make love to her friend if he would be willing to watch. She went on to make sure he knew that this was for his pleasure and that she loved him with all if her heart. He put his hands on her face and kissed her in a way that allowed their tongues to dance in each other's mouth. He ran his fingers through her hair as he told her how much he loves her.

She didn't introduce her friend because she wasn't going to be coming back again, this was the only time they would see each other.

The three of them went to the bedroom and she had him sit in the chair at the foot of the bed. She handed him a towel anticipating that he was going to want to feel the need to massage his shaft as things got exciting.

She turned the lights down low with enough light he could see what they were doing but not too much light so you could see any imperfections.

The two women stood close and undressed themselves down to their bra and panties. They removed their bras at the same time and when their firm breasts were exposed you could hear the gasp in the room. Arrangements had been made so the friend knew to be the submissive one in the role playing and allow her to take the lead. They each reached out and grabbed each other's breast, massaging and pulling lightly on the nipples. She moved towards the friend, bent down slightly, and took her friends nipple into her mouth. The friend tilted her head back and let out a light scream of "yes". The sound of satisfaction just made her suckle more firmly and massage at the same time. She reaches down between her friends legs and was pleased to feel the warm moisture that had collected on her sweet bud. She lightly stroked between her swollen lips and gathered some of that juice onto her fingers. She released her friends' nipple and wiped the juices onto her friends' lips and then kissed her lips as the two enjoyed the flavor. Her friend reached for her hand and sucked the last of the juices off those sweet fingers.

She then gave her friend a light tap to indicate she wanted her to lie back on the bed. Now that she has had a taste of her sweet nectar she wanted more.

She spread her friends' legs, spread her sweet lips apart and slid her tongue past the moisture hole and across her swelling clit. Her hips rose slightly as she let out a deep moan. She did this same move two more times and the reaction was stronger each time. She knew she was ready and she lifted her legs and with them spread she pressed them against her friends' chest. There it was, her friends beautiful asshole. She dipped two fingers into her warm wet honey pot and then smeared those juices along the rim of that tight asshole.

Her friend moved away slightly so she leaned over her as she massaged her ass, relax sweetie, you are going to love this, trust me.

One she had her friends sweet juices spread around that sweet ass she leaned over, spread her friends cheeks apart and then began to lick the inside of those cheeks. Her friends' ass still high in the air she was able to lick from her sweet pussy all along her path to that tight ass. After licking that path a few times she took her tongue and licked all around that ass, pulling her cheeks apart so she could get her tongue firmly on that sweet hole and the darting her tongue into her ass. Her friend let out a loud moan of pleasure and instead of pulling away she pressed her ass against her face. She was enjoying how this felt, nobody had ever done this to her before. Her knees were a little weak but she stayed firm, wanting more of this wonderful licking.

Taking her tongue going down she pulled more sweet juices from that honey pot. She coated her tongue with the warm, wet, and silky cum. She spreads her friends' cheeks apart, slides her tongue from the juices dripping from her friends flower and making her way to that tight sweet ass hole. Her tongue circles that virgin hole and then, she squeezes her ample cheeks and firmly darts her tongue inside. Her friend lets out a high pitched yell of excitement. Her boyfriend moans with desire as he watches from his chair. The noises in the room make her want to continue and she becomes a bit more aggressive. Slapping her friends' ass in a playful way as her tongue continues to lick that sweet crack and licks around the rim before darting in.

She moves her hand between the legs of her friend and slides her thumb into that wet box. While she massages her inner walls her finger glides over her firm flower. She lifts her head slightly and sees her man with his pants down, slowly stroking his long thick shaft.

With her thumb moving faster against her walls she feels her muscles pulsing. She was about to release another orgasm.

She leaned forward and whispered in her friends' ear, "I will give you one more orgasm. Cover my hand with your cum and then you need to leave so I can take care of my man". It was what they had agreed on before this evening began. Secretly, she hoped to be able to do this again but have the two of them please her man in a different way.

She pressed he'd thumb firmly against her smooth inner wall. With her index and middle finger, she glided over her budding flower as her tongue darting into her sweet ass. Her friend started to buck slightly, forcing her thumb in deeper and she moaned out that she was about to cum. Then she ore moved her thumb from her warm juices and pressed it into that sweet tight ass. It was an instant moan of pleasure from her friend. Her friend then arched her back tilted her head and the orgasm hit. She helped her friend release by pushing her thumb in and out as he friend bucked with pleasure. Screams of YES . . . YES . . . YES were heard as her friends' entire body started to pulse and then shake. She slowly pulled her thumb out of that nice hole. She leaned against her friends back and gave her a firm hug. They both stood up, pressed their naked bodies together, kissed, and her friend picked up her clothes and left the room.

She was now alone with her man who was still slowly stroking that beautiful cock of his. She quickly washed her hands so she could take that cock into her hands. She went over to him, hissed him deeply, her legs straddled his leg, her warm juices dripping onto his leg until she squatted down and pressed her moistness against his leg as she slid back and forth.

He reached up and massaged her breasts. She reached down to take his shaft in her hand. She doesn't remember it ever being that firm before. It was the stiffest his shaft has ever been and it felt incredible to her.

Watching her play with the ass of her friend made her man very hot and he now wanted to take her sweet ass and make it his.

He stood up, grabbed the hair at the back of her head, and pulled her head back. He kissed her with passion, moaning as his tongue darted into her mouth. As he was kissing her he decided he was going to take control. He pulled away from her, gave her ass a firm slap, grabbed her arm to turn her around and pushed her towards the bed. As she started to walk, she stopped to turn around because she wanted more kisses but he stopped her. He made it clear that he was in charge, he was in control and he slapped her ass again. He guided her towards the bed.

WALK AT THE RESERVOIR

It was a beautiful day for a walk and I met my Master at a trail at the Reservoir. I could tell by the look on his face that he was surprised and pleased to see that I arrived wearing a skirt. As I walked closer to him, he extended his arm. I knew what he wanted so I turned slightly as I got closer and he grabbed my hair in a way that reminded me of his power. With force he pulled my head back and with his other hand he firmly grabs that firm breast, the breast that belongs to him. I took a deep breath as he grabbed that breast and pulled it up and out of my shirt where his lips met that firm nipple instantly. He released my hair and pulled me closer so he could give that breast even more attention. All I can say is I wish I was wearing panties that could absorb at least some of the moisture that was about to be released.

He stopped suddenly and with his hand at the small of my back he pushed me lightly and we started to walk down the trail. He asked if I was sorry for the problems I caused by the assignment I had given to him. The answer: "no". I wasn't sorry; I was excited to know that my words could make him throb. I honestly thought he should be praising me for writing something that turned him on so much.

He grabbed my left arm, turned me around and firmly said . . ."The smell of your hair, the way the wind blows it, you have done it again, my cock needs attention . . . NOW". I looked at him and smiled and we walked off the path to a more secluded location and I began to unbuckle and unzip his slacks. Oooh, how beautiful. The velvet like tip so smooth and there is a drop of moisture just waiting to be licked off. I don't even ask for permission as I take the tip to my lips and my tongue slides over the tip. My hand firmly at the base, I am not going to let go until I have finished this task.

"Wait, stop right NOW" he orders. "Look up at me" My eyes look up to see his face as I held that beautiful tip next to my lips and I continued to stroke it from the base to the tip. "You are **not** to cum. This walk is for my pleasure only. You caused me problems with your last assignment; I told you there would be consequences. Stand up and let me feel that pussy, it better be dry right now and it better stay that way". I held back the tear. He had not asked me to stay dry before. I was hoping he would rethink the need to punish me. He slowly slides his hand up my inner thigh, his finger gliding between my swollen lips. I closed my eyes and hoped he didn't go in deep enough to touch my clit because I knew that one light touch and I was going to cum on his hand right then. "Good Girl, now stay dry for me" he said with a smile. Phew, that was close!

He sat down on a log; I knelt down in front of him. My mouth opened wide as I took that long firm shaft into my mouth. With skill, using one hand to stroke the shaft as my mouth worked to suck the juice from him. The other hand rubbing just at the base of his jewels. My tongue moving strategically along the shaft flicking the underside just before the ridge of the tip. My mouth warm for him, gliding up and down the shaft. I have to slow down; I can feel my pussy starting to pulse. I don't think I can make it; I have to concentrate to prevent my own explosion. As I slow down he grabs my head and starts to thrust into my mouth, I resist, I can't hold back my orgasm. I pull my mouth off of him, look him in his eyes and beg for permission. "Master, I beg of you, please let me release. I can't resist it any longer, I am about to explode." He looked at me, gave my hair a strong yank, and said very firmly: "NO, get back to your assignment. Pull the juices from me, I will feed you. **Maybe** after I have been taken care of we can talk about your needs. **MAYBE**".

This wasn't going to be easy. I stroked that firm shaft and wrapped my lips around the tip and I started back up. Gliding up and down until I felt the tip hitting the back of my throat. He can feel the vibration on his shaft as I moan with pleasure. I can tell he is enjoying it, his shaft is starting to pulse and he is close to feeding me. But, I don't know if I can hold off my own orgasm. Then, it happens, he firmly grabs my shoulders . . . he is about to release. My breathing becomes heavy. His pulsing is faster, the throbbing firmer. I look up at him, he arches his back slightly and he fills my mouth and I drink it with honor and respect.

I did it; I was able to hold back my own orgasm. I haven't been forced to stay dry for a long time; I didn't think I could do it that day. He pulls me up and slowly slides his hand up my skirt. His finger glides between my swollen lips, looks into my eyes and smiles. "You did good. You have remembered your training. Pull your skirt up, lie down on the ground in front of me and force yourself to release. Let me watch you." I quickly did as instructed and he watched my every move. As my orgasm got closer he saw my pussy pulsing and my hips moving up and down faster. He got down on the ground with me, his face deep between my legs and I fed him that afternoon." Both of us had the smell of cum on our faces, it was the best walk on the trails that I ever experienced. We were both marked with each other's scent. We would stop at a local business and share a bathroom so we could wash each other clean.

HIS PLEASURE

I lay before you, legs spread wide, and this pussy that belongs to you is ready for inspection, Master. Please rub that velvet tip across those ripe and swollen lips and watch that clit grow firm for you. I reach to touch that beautiful cock and you quickly slap me firmly on the thigh and with a stern tone you tell me to lay still for inspection. You remind me that you have not given me permission to touch you yet.

You get up and open the drawer where you keep all of your tools. You pull out the blindfold and order me to put it on. Putting me into darkness and order me to lie on my back and spread my legs wide. I beg you not to out me into darkness. I remind you about how much I dislike this activity, I love the way you look and want to see your body in front of me.

You give me a firm slap on my inner thigh. You tell me to hush and remind me that I will do as you say—like it or not. You give my inner thigh a firm smack and I gasp and start to move my legs together but your quickly gab them and spread them back apart. Three sharp slaps on my inner thigh and I begin to apologize for attempting to put my legs together. I know I've done wrong and the warmth from his slaps is a reminder that I've done wrong.

Now you begin the inspection. With my legs spread wide you pull the outer lips apart exposing the sweet pink clit. You flick the clit and watch as it gets firmer for you. Then you spread the inner lips apart to expose the warm wet honey pot. You press one finger inside and circles the inner walls. Feeling the smoothness and you then add a second finger. You can tell by the way I am biting my lip that I am enjoying this activity. I gasp as you press firmly on the inner wall. You remind me that I am not allowed to cum until you give permission to do so. You feel the walls of the pussy grabbing your fingers as I work hard to stop the orgasm you started to create. At that moment you pull your fingers out and step back.

As the touching stops, I ask: "What are you doing, Master? Please tell me what you are doing." I try to listen for noises in hopes I can tell what is about to happen but the music is turned up too loud, I can't tell what is going on.

I feel you pull those swollen lips apart to expose that firm clit. My breathing becomes heavy; your touch has electrified me. Smack, you give that clit a firm slap. Again . . . Again . . . Again. I speak: "use me Master, I belong to you, use me for your pleasure". You start to rub that clit with your thumb. Then I feel it, the warm drop of the candle wax. First one, then another. My body jumps just a little on the second drop, it was much hotter than the first. I let out a light moan of pain and pleasure. A third drop hit and was instantly followed by the touch of an ice cube. My hips rose because of the shock, not knowing what was happening. A scream of pleasure is heard from me. I want to beg to have the blindfold removed but I know I shouldn't yet. You continue to hold the ice onto the clit and I can feel that it is starting to numb the area a bit. You seem to know exactly when to stop holding the ice there and you slip it down into the honey pot where it melts almost instantly. Again, I let out a pleasure moan.

You give that clit a slap again and then you squeeze it between your fingers. You give me permission to totally enjoy what you are doing to me. I can feel it, the pulsing begins, and you know what you are doing. I am hoping that you will make me squirt for you . . . like the Master that you are you make it happen. Just as I am about to squirt for you, you remove the blindfold. You want to see my eyes when you make me squirt. I let out a scream of pleasure as it happens; my hips start to move up and down. In a very firm tone you order me to be still . . . to stop moving.

Your cock is hard; moisture has collected at the tip. You straddle my face and slap me with that hard cock. I open my mouth, I want to taste it but you avoid my mouth totally. My hands grab your nice ass in hopes I can get you to move that hard cock closer to my mouth. You grab my hair; pull me up so I am sitting up. You stand before me, hands still firmly grabbing my hair and you guide your cock across my lips. You order me to open my mouth and stick out my tongue as you slide your cock across my cheeks you slap your hard cock against my tongue.

You order me to take our cock into my mouth. "Suck that cock butch, make it cum for you". My tongue glides over the tip then my lips wrap around the ridge of your shaft. Then you hold onto my head while you fuck my mouth. Yelling at me to suck the cum from you. Then, when your orgasm builds and you are about to fill my mouth you remind me that i must swallow every drop. I am not allowed to waste a drop, "Swallow bitch, don't waste a drop, suck it all out of me".

After licking your cock clean you praise me for a job well done. I passed inspection today and my Master is pleased.

LOYALTY

The day became an incredible day when she found out that there was going to be an opportunity to take care of her Master. After hearing that in some countries the servants sucked on their King's nipples to show their loyalty all she could think about was having a chance to treat her Master like a King. She wanted to show her loyalty. She had thought about it for days and she was going to get her chance. Oh, how she looked forward to pleasing him in a King's fashion.

They arrived at the location. She was wearing a skirt with s sexy tank top covered with a work appropriate jacket. Her breathing was heavy with anticipation. Her panties already damp and then he exposed his beautiful chest to her, nipples nice and firm. He gave her the ok to move closer and she was certainly ready. Her mouth open, her tongue glides across that firm nipple, her mouth opens and she begins to suckle. Her right hand moves over to his other nipple and begins to massage and gently tugging on his nipple. She would lick his nipple and then go back to firmly sucking. Licking and sucking his nipples was pushing her to the edge, she came several times as she was building up to a full orgasm.

He voiced his pleasure with what she was doing and that made her want it even more. She can feel his strength when he speaks. "That's it, oooh mmmy, that's it. You do know what you are doing; you are making your Master, your King, very happy. Yeah, keep it up babe, don't stop. Suck that tit" He grabbed her hair in his hands and began to pull firmly but never strong enough to pull her mouth off of his firm tight nipple. The combination of his voice and the pulling of her hair was about to take her over the edge.

Hey . . . what was that? She didn't see that coming. He slapped her pussy and since she was so close to an orgasm she felt that slap deep inside her core. Again and again, he kept firmly slapping her. "Spread your legs, bitch, open it up to me. That pussy belongs to me spread those legs". She complied instantly but never left his nipple. Her legs spread wide, pussy totally exposed for him. Each slap a little harder than the last. The juices were starting to flow, as he slapped that pussy the juices splattered. The smell of sex filled the room.

She continued sucking his nipple feeling it get firmer against her tongue. His other nipple, between her fingers, was nice and firm. She felt his pleasure when she pulled gently on his nipple followed by a slight nibble and a firm sucking on the other. He pulled more firmly on her hair, she knew he was pleased. She felt her juices flowing and that big orgasm was so very close, she was about to explode but she was trying hard to hold it. She didn't want this to end.

She reached down and gently rubbed his cock that was still hidden from her inside his slacks. She could feel it was hard and she could feel a slight wet spot on his jeans. "That's it bitch, feel how hard that cock is for you. Don't stop sucking that nipple. You better keep that cock rock hard for you". When he talks to her with the stern voice she gets so excited. She can't believe that a man with his power has picked her to be his slave.

She grabbed his cock a little firmer as her body shook; she wasn't going to be able to hold it back. She grabbed onto his shoulder, pressed her mouth more firmly against his nipple, she was going to cum. She became more aggressive, another small orgasm hit. She could feel the slick moisture building. She tugged more firmly on his nipple, grabbed his shoulder tightly . . . she had to pull her mouth off of his nipple, this orgasm was strong and it took over her entire body for that moment. He knew her so very well and knew what was about to happen. He knew exactly when the timing was right as he quickly shoved, with some force, 2 of his fingers deep inside that slippery wet pussy. Her body pulsed, started to ride his fingers, she screamed out; "this is for you Master, this orgasm belongs to you". Her pussy grabbed his fingers and throbbed firmly against them as she rode out the orgasm for her Master. As soon as it passed she went right back. Licking, sucking, licking, and sucking. Her King deserved this treatment, she was so glad that he was enjoying it.

It was time; he was ready to feed her. He ordered her to sit back as he pulled out his beautiful, long, hard cock. She licked her lips, she was ready. He put his hand on the back of her head, grabbing her hair as he pushed her head down onto the tip of his cock. She wrapped her lips around the tip and he pushed her head down. "Take it, suck that cock bitch. That's it, ride it". He was ready to cum, she had pulled him close to an orgasm as she sucked his nipple and he was going to cum quickly. Then he announce . . ."**That's it, that's it, take it . . . take all of it**" and he fed her his warm juices. As soon as she felt her mouth fill she felt her own orgasm hit again.

She sat up to swallow the rest of the juices, she turned to go down on him again to lick off the rest of the juices but he was already putting that beautiful shaft away. Her breathing got heavy again when she saw that last drop on the tip – he saw the look in her eye as he gave his shaft a slight stroke forcing the last of the juices out the tip. He caught the juices on his finger, turned to her, and insisted she expose her breasts for him NOW. She pulled both breasts out and he spread those juices between them. He announced to her, "wear my scent proudly, you have been marked by me, you belong to me now".

She put her breasts back into her shirt ever so carefully so the juices would have a chance to dry against her skin. She bowed her head, glanced up at him and said . . . "I belong to you now, Sir. Thank you." She just couldn't believe that she was finally able to treat him like a King and is looking forward to doing it again. Her legs were a little weak from the multiple orgasms he pulled from her. He is a great Master, he treats her well.

PLEASE SPANK ME

She has a dilemma, there is something she would like to ask for but there really isn't a place that it could be done. She finally decided to say something; maybe he would like it too. If not, she was so very satisfied with the adventures they were enjoying at this point. She has felt his power; she enjoyed his firmness and often thinks about the firmness he has shown her. He was a good Master, she won't complain.

But, the truth was she really wanted to be spanked firmly. The kind of spanking that would make her sweet ass red. Then, when that sweet ass is a nice shade of red – get out the cell phone and take a picture so she can look at it regularly and be reminded of his firmness, his power. But, then again, this would require her to show him something that is outside of her comfort zone.

She knew she would do it, for him, if that would please him.

He smiled lightly when she told him of her dirty little secret but it wasn't mentioned ever again after she brought it up. She wasn't concerned, her Master provides her with several orgasms every week, he allows her to suckle on his nipples, and he feeds her regularly, she is very happy to serve her Master, her King. Not to mention the flow of sweet juices while she sits at her desk and releases for him regularly. Secretly she doesn't know what she would do if he ever asked that she stay dry, she doesn't think she could do it because just thinking of his power makes her wet. Then, once she feels that silky smooth moisture between the lips protecting her honey pot she just wants more.

It happened one rainy day when he sent her the text. The message simply read: "I will pick you up at the front door in 5 minutes. Wait for me there." She was confused by the message; he never picks her up, she always drives to the destination. She later found out that he didn't want her to have to run out in the rain to get to her car. He does take good care of his slave.

She jumped into his vehicle as soon as he pulled to the front of the building. Once she got in he looked at her and said, with firmness, "reach up your shirt and start to pull on your nipples. I want you to be one horny bitch when we arrive at our destination". She looked at him as if to question his request. "Now. Do not delay. Start pulling on them NOW"!! YES, the power, her pussy started to pulse instantly, her breathing heavy, she enjoys hearing the power in his voice she was very excited. He watched her tugging on her nipples through the corner of his eyes. As he turned into the park she arched her back, she was going to be his horny bitch. As they started to drive down that narrow drive, he instructed her to pull her tits out of her shirt and pull firmly on her nipples in plain view. This was going to make her his horny bitch and make him her horny Master, her horny King.

She was sure they would stay in the vehicle because of the rain so as soon as they parked she turned to him and started to reach for his nipples. He stopped her and pushed her hand away. "Today **your** desires will be taken care of" he said with kindness. You've been good to me; I want to watch you praise me with delight.

He had a large umbrella and he held it over her so they could walk to the men's room. This was the place where they had their very first encounter. He slapped her sweet ass firmly as she got out of the vehicle. As soon they entered the room he quickly slapped her sweet ass again. She stood up straight and let out a gasp. He grabbed her arm and turned her as he slapped her sweet ass again. "I am going to make that ass red today. You have been a good and loyal slave. You have served me well and I know you are going to like this. You asked for something to remind you of my power and today you will have pictures of my power". He kept spanking that ass but did allow her to move closer and he exposed his chest to her. She quickly moved close enough to give him the treatment of a King. As she sucked and pulled on his nipples he would grab her hair and pull her mouth away so he could get in a few more very firm and solid slaps on that sweet ass of hers. With each slap, as soon as he released her hair, she went to his nipple and sucked more firmly than before. Each slap made her hornier than before. She could feel her ass start to burn, she could feel his power, she was so turned on she could hardly stand up to take care of his needs.

His cock was starting to twitch. She was doing her job well and he liked how it was making him feel. She was taking him to the point where he wanted to feed her. "Drop your pants, NOW. Let me see that I have adequately marked that ass of yours". She did as instructed and did not question. She could tell he was serious. She was very uncomfortable because being even partially nude like that is outside of her comfort zone. He reached towards her, his hand between her legs. He felt the moisture as she let out a light moan as she tried to grind onto his hand. Her hand reached out and gave his nipple a firm squeeze.

With his hand on the back of her head, he pushed her over so she was bent over and her ass was right there for the proper slapping. He pulled that beautiful, hard cock out of his slacks and started to slap her ass with it. Alternating, his cock, his hand, and then repeating the process. He was losing fluids and it was splattering across her ass, she could feel the warmth. She began to let out a light moan with each slap, her ass was feeling the heat, and she felt his power right then. He quickly snaps a couple pictures of that red hot ass, and then he lays his cock across the cheek of her ass and takes another picture. Her body starting to twitch, she was going to cum hard any second. One last picture as he lays his cock between her ass cheeks. She couldn't be quiet any longer, she wanted to cum hard. "Please, Master, bring me that cock. Feed me. Allow me to cum with you. I beg of you, let me taste your warm nectar. Please, Master, I beg you to feed me." He took his cock in one hand, opened the lips on her pussy with the other and slid that firm cock across her swollen pussy and covered it in the juices she had just lost.

With a gentle voice he replies, "Come here and drink this. Hurry, my pet, I am about to shoot this all over your ass if you don't hurry. I would hate to see it wasted" With her mouth open she turns towards him. He grabs her head, pushes his cock into her mouth and feeds her promptly. As he said; "yes, that's it, take it, take all of it, all of it, and suck me dry . . . oohhh, yyyessss, that's it. You've got it". She grabs onto his hips as he fills her mouth. He looks down, her eyes closed, his cock in her mouth and he takes a picture.

Both very satisfied they returned to the vehicle to head back to their jobs. As they got to the vehicle, she turned to her Master, reached over and ran her hand across his chest and smiled as she said to him . . ."Thank you Sir. I belong to you". With a smile he simply replied; "yes you do".

He then let her know that he will contact her soon and the next encounter will be dedicated to his pleasure only. She will serve him like a good bitch when he calls. She showed him your loyalty, her dedication, she will be tested again soon and he is sure his bitch will be ready to submit to his desires.

Later on she opens her pictures so she can file them in a spot that nobody else can access, to keep them private. She will send them to their personal account where only they can see them. That was when she saw the proof of how beautifully red he had made her sweet ass, she will cherish those pictures and use them to take her to a hard orgasm when her Master is not available. Then she saw the pictures of his cock across her ass and she saw the glistening moisture on the tip. She slid her fingers between her legs and started to massage her pulsing clit, her breathing became heavy. Then, she saw the last picture . . . her mouth full of cock. She was not going to stop massaging her pussy until she came hard. When the orgasm hit, even though she was alone, she moaned out praises to her Master. That orgasm belonged to him.

Created with honor and respect for her Master

SUMMONED

She was summoned to report to his home at 9:00am on Saturday. She was anxious and excited because he had been fighting a cold so they have not seen each other for several days. This must indicate he is feeling better and that makes her smile. She was sure to put Ina fresh blade on her razor so she was as smooth as possible when they meet.

Saturday finally arrived and she was preparing to head to his home. She had showered and was careful not to allow herself to get excited. She wanted to make sure her body was sensitive and would be reactive to his touch. It had been several days since she has released an orgasm; she hopes he will be pleased.

She took a deep breath and pressed the button for the doorbell at his place. He answered the door wearing jeans and no shirt. He took her hand and led her in past the door. She smiled widely when she saw him. Remove your coat, my pet, and let me see if you followed your directions. She knew this indicated that there would be no foreplay and he wanted to get down to business. She loosened the belt on her coat and opened the front, let it fall off her shoulders, and then completely removed it for his inspection. She knew he would be pleased to find she was wearing nothing under her coat. Her nipples firm with desire.

He reached out and grabbed each of her breasts firmly, pinched and tugged on each nipple and watched as her chest began to rise as her breathing became heavy. She so enjoys his touch and her entire body was reacting. He took her face in his hand by pressing his thumb on one side of her jaw and his index finger on the other side. He kissed her deeply and then, while still holding her face and forcing her to look into his eyes he asked her if she was ready to give herself to him totally. She responded with a simple, "yes, Sir. I belong to you, Sir." At that moment he gave her right breast a firm slap, turned her around and gave her ass three firm, sharp, slaps and he said, "good. Go to the pleasure room my slut and I want you to stop on every fourth step you take and bend over so I can see that wet pussy glisten".

She began to walk towards the pleasure room and, as instructed, stopped on every fourth step she took. She spread her legs slightly as she bent over; he was quick to slide his fingers from her firm clit dragging moisture to her tight asshole. He gave her permission to stand and begin to move forward. This process was repeated 4 times until she arrived in the pleasure room. During the last time she bent over he surprised her by quickly sliding two fingers deep inside her warm, wet, pussy and he trust in and out several times. When he pulled his fingers out he gave her ass three firm sharp slaps. She started to stand before he instructed her to do so and he firmly placed his hand on her shoulder and pressed back down to her bent over position. With a firm told he said; "I didn't tell you to stand yet, bitch." As she was bent back down he spread her ass cheeks apart and she spit, with precision, onto her hole. He rubbed his spit around the rim before he slid his middle finger deep inside her. As he was moving his finger in and out he reminded her that she needed to learn discipline. What he didn't know was that even though it was a firm punishment she was enjoying what he was doing to her. She kept quiet and stayed bent over until he instructed her to stand up.

When she was instructed to do so that was when she saw it. Something new in the room, he had installed a very nice leather strap swing. He took her near the swing and he helped her get into the swing. First putting her legs into the opening and slid those straps and tightened them on her upper thighs and smoothed the straps to ensure comfort. Then he helped her get her arms strapped in. He sat her down and then began to raise the swing. He pushed her back until so she was in a reclined and relaxed position. As the swing was raised to a height perfect for his pleasure; she held onto the leather straps so when he had her raised up her legs were spread wide, legs dangling at her knees. Her body totally exposed for his inspection, ready to be used for his pleasure. He walks over to her, kisses her with passion then he tells her that he will allow her to keep her hands free if she can keep them up with her hands holding firmly on the swing and she agreed. However, he did out a blindfold over her eyes and there was no negotiation on his decision to do that.

He firmly grabbed her right breast and then her left. He pinched each nipple so firmly that her back arched and she left out a very loud moan. He was quick to tell her to be quiet. Reminding her that she needs to hush.

Then he gave each breast a slap so sharp her breast was warm and red. She couldn't help herself, she let out a soft scream and her hands quickly came down and she massaged her breasts to ease the pain. She knew the instant that she did that she would be punished and she quickly raised her hands to grab the swing as she repeatedly apologized for her actions.

Quietly he walked behind her and tied her hands to the swing so she won't be able to lower them until he was ready for her to do that. As he was securing her to the swing she was begging him not to do it but he said nothing. As he tightened the last strap to secure her, he pressed his index finger against her lips as he simply said "shhhhh, you need to be quiet. You can't be allowed the freedom of your hands at this time". With her eyes covered she couldn't tell where he had gone or what he was planning next. Then she felt his breath near her face. He kissed her softly several times. Then she felt it and several tears dripped from below the blindfold and she began to beg him not to do it. She knew what she felt was a ball gag and that was one thing she really hated. She doesn't like anything that blocks her airway, she knows he would never hurt her but this brings out her claustrophobic fears. She reluctantly opened her mouth and he placed the ball gag firmly into her mouth.

He pressed on her forehead to lean her back so she would allow the swing to support her head and release some of the strain from her neck. He kissed her face, kissed her neck, kept kissing his way down between her breasts. He could feel that she was relaxing and knew that she could begin to enjoy what he had planned.

He walked over to the table where he had his toys. He grabbed his crop with the long leather strips on the end. He walked around her, she could hear is footsteps and then she felt it as he crop gently hit her abdomen and slid across her stomach in a ticklish way. Then he firmly grabbed her breast. The leather strips then hit her breast but this time firmer than the last hit. With the gag in her mouth she can only moan. He started to walk around her slapping that crop against her randomly. Slapping on her breasts, abdomen, upper thighs, feet, and across her pussy from the top and also coming up from under her. Each hit made he moan and he continued to walk around her a second time. Stopping to grab her breast and a couple times he grabbed her breast and wrapped his lips around her nipple and would suckle while still slapping her with the crop. He so loved her large firm nipples.

It was time to move on; he went to the table and picked up a vibrating egg. He walked towards her and placed it on her nipple before turning it on. She began moaning with joy as she felt that vibration. "Oh, you like that don't you? Your nipples are showing signs of excitement bitch" he repeated as he rubbed that egg across her breasts. He would slap her breast every now and then just to keep her on her toes. He moved that vibrator down her abdomen and he spread her legs as he slid that vibrator between her legs but was careful to stay away from her clit. He could see that it was firm and he didn't want her to release yet. With her legs spread he would blow onto her clit just to watch it pulse for him. He couldn't resist and he did go between her legs to kiss those lips. Then he walked around her and kissed her mouth. He slapped her breast before he went back to his table.

This time he grabbed two short round candles, lit them, and placed them between her toes. As he gave her instructions that she needed to be careful not to move and spill the waiting candle wax. He walked around her once without touching her. She heard his footsteps and she wondered when he would touch her. Then he stopped, she took a deep breath in anticipation and he grabbed her breast and began to suckle her nipple. She had to concentrate so she didn't move her legs and spill the wax. She arched her back and she couldn't help but rock her hips a little. He knew how much she loved this move; he knew it would be difficult for her to keep her legs steady. While suckling her nipple his hand went between her legs and she let out as much of a scream as she could with the gag in her mouth. He stood up and laughed as he said, "Oh my bitch, you are struggling but doing so very well. I do enjoy watching you struggle."

He went down to her feet and grabbed the candles, both with melted wax pooled at the too. As he walked around her he spilled wax lightly across her abdomen, her chest and on her inner thighs. With each drip she twisted a little and let out a scream of surprise.

He flicked each nipple with his finger as he inspected her body, confirming she had been waxed properly. As he was walking around her he was releasing his growing shaft. As he neared her head he reached up and removed the blind fold kissing her eyelids as they are exposed. Then he removed the ball gag and kissed her mouth as soon as the ball was removed. Then he reached up and released her hands and massaged her wrists as soon as the straps were removed. She looked at him and quietly thanked him. When he heard her sweet voice he kissed her with deep passion.

He lowered her swing a little and placed his shaft against her mouth, pre cum covered his tip. He instructed her to lick off the pre cum and then to take that sweet cock deep into her mouth. She was still laying back in the swing and he began to fuck her warm mouth watching as every inch of his shaft went into her mouth. The way she massaged his shaft with her mouth was going to pull the cum out of him but this isn't where he wanted it released so he quickly pulled out.

He walked down between her legs, spread them wide and adjusted the swing so bit her glistening pussy and her tight ass were accessible. He started by rubbing the tip of his shaft between her swollen lips pressing lightly against her firm clit. Up and down, slowly at first and then faster and faster. Her hips moving up and down and she begins to beg him to fuck her. Her legs begin to tighten because the orgasm is so close. He slips inside her slowly. He enjoys watching her pussy take in his shaft slowly. The way her lips wrapped around his shaft and how she tried to pull him in. When each inch was fully inside her and the tip pressed deep inside her walls he began to thrust, his hands on her hips to provide stability with each thrust.

This wasn't where he wanted to leave his cum so he pulled his shaft out before it was too late. He reached over to grab the lube he placed nearby. With a small dollop on his finger he rubbed it on her waiting rim. He rubbed the tip of his cock with that lube and pressed the tip at her opening. He's angled her in the swing so he can watch his hard shaft enter her. He starts to press the tip into her. He reminds her to take a deep breath as he pressed harder. Her hole spreading for him, she moans softly as he presses the head in and she lets out a sign of relief as the head is inside just past his defined rim. He rubs a little lube on his shaft that hasn't yet entered her. He announces, "oh, baby, this is beautiful, is wish you could see this as my cock starts to enter you and how your ass stretches for me." She asks him if he can reach his cell online and video it for her. He had a camera installed when he had the swing out in and he had been recording, she just didn't know it yet. He began to move in and out of her tight ass and picked up the pace when she was relaxed and enjoying it. His body tightened up as his cock started to pulse. He began to cum and he pulled his cock out so he could squirt his fluids at the rim of her hole and he then watched as it slowly dripped back onto her hole.

He lowered the swing and helped her release the straps. As she stood up he pressed his body against hers as he told her what a great bitch she was for him. She thanked him and he returned the thanks to her. They stood there holding each other for several minutes before they moved to the bathroom to clean up.